D1243648

fresh
& local

WITHDRAWN

Craig Flinn

Formac Publishing Company Limited

To a father, from a grateful son

Formac Publishing Company Limited acknowledges the support of the Cultural Affairs Section, Nova Scotia Department of Tourism, Culture and Heritage. We acknowledge the financial support of the Government of Canada through the Book Publishing Industry Development Program (BPIDP) for our publishing activities.

NOVA SCOTIA
Tourism, Culture and Heritage

Library and Archives Canada Cataloguing in Publication
Flinn, Craig
      Fresh & local : straight from Canadian farms to your table / Craig
Flinn ; foreword by Michael Smith.
ISBN 978-0-88780-743-5
      1. Cookery — Nova Scotia. 2. Cookery, Canadian — Nova Scotia style.
3. Cookery, Canadian, — Maritime style. 4. Local foods — Nova Scotia.
5. Local foods — Maritime Provinces. I. Title. II. Title: Fresh and local.
TX715.6.F55 2008   641.59716   C2008-903847-9

Formac Publishing Company Limited
5502 Atlantic Street
Halifax, Nova Scotia B3H 1G4
www.formac.ca

Printed in China

Contents

Seasons

Within each chapter, the recipes are categorized by season to help you make the most out of fresh and locally produced fruits, vegetables, meats, fish and artisan food products. The following colours highlight when the recipe ingredients are freshest and most readily available from local sources. As an additional reference, the Seasonal Recipe Index (pg. 184) will let you shift your cooking selections with the seasons.

spring

summer

fall

winter

Smoked Yukon Gold Potato Chowder with Seared Arctic Char

This unique chowder base is fantastic with any seafood, but I have recently discovered incredible organic, farm-raised Arctic char in Nova Scotia that works particularly well. If you can't find Arctic char in your area, use wild salmon or farm-raised trout instead. If you do not want to go to the trouble of smoking the potatoes, use a tablespoon of liquid smoke, available at most grocery stores.

Soup
1 ½ lb (700 g) Yukon Gold potatoes, peeled and quartered
1 cup (250 mL) maple, apple or hickory wood chips
1 cup (250 mL) diced onion
½ cup (125 mL) chopped celery
1 cup (250 mL) sliced leek (white part only)
3 cloves garlic
2 tsp (10 mL) salt
2 tsp (10 mL) white pepper
¼ cup (60 mL) butter
½ cup (125 mL) white wine
6 cups (1.5 L) chicken broth
1 cup (250 mL) heavy cream (35% m.f.)

Seared Arctic Char
1 lb (450 g) Arctic char fillets, cut into 8 x 2-oz (60-g) pieces
3 tbsp (45 mL) olive oil
chives, for garnish
extra-virgin olive oil, for garnish

Using a barbecue or stove-top smoker, smoke potatoes over high heat for five minutes once the wood chips begin to smoke.

In a medium stockpot, sauté onion, celery, leeks, garlic, salt and pepper in butter until translucent. Deglaze the pot with white wine and reduce by half. Add potatoes, broth and cream and simmer for 90 minutes. Purée in a well-vented blender, strain into a clean saucepan and keep warm on a low burner.

Preheat a nonstick frying pan and sear char pieces in a little olive oil. Season with salt and pepper.

To serve, portion chowder into hot bowls and place 2 pieces of char in the centre of each bowl. Garnish with sliced chives and a drizzle of extra-virgin olive oil and, if you are adventurous, homemade potato chips.

Serves 4, with some leftover soup for the next day

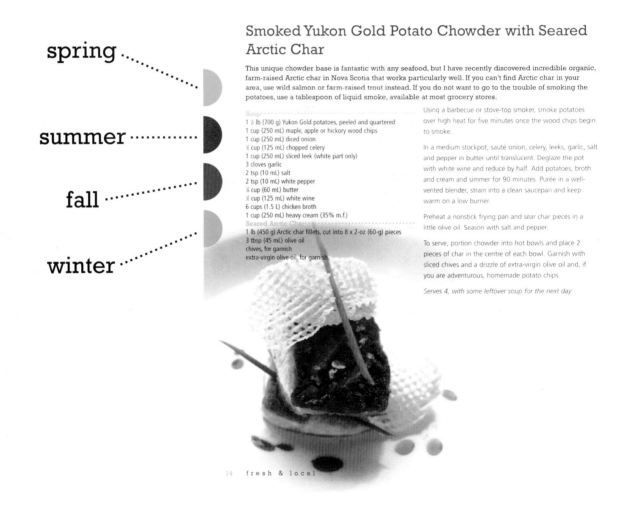

14   fresh & local

Foreword

There are few food experiences as memorable as that moment at Chives when you first open their beautiful little paper bags of freshly baked chive biscuits and inhale the aroma of Chef Craig Flinn's cooking genius. As the story goes the bag and the biscuits were a frantic last minute fill-in conceived on the day the restaurant opened as a way to "get some bread on the table." Those simple biscuits, humbly presented in a brown paper bag, have gone on to become a signature of the restaurant and a hallmark of Craig's style.

Chef Craig Flinn is one of Canada's leading chefs but at heart he is still just a cook. The sort of cook who understands that food may be prepared in the kitchen but it comes alive at the table. Craig's instinctive hospitality, his love of sharing, his burning desire to show off the best of his Nova Scotia roots are all fully realized in that simple moment when you bite into one of his biscuits. What better way to start your meal in a restaurant so firmly rooted in the flavours and traditions of our collective home?

In recent years Canada's cuisine has rightly taken its place on the global table as one of the most exciting and vibrant examples of what cooking can be when chefs and farmers sit at the same table. In Craig's hands our national culinary identity is strong and flavourful yet humble and grounded at the same time. He cooks food that we instinctively understand, flavours that we crave, food that is somehow simultaneously creative and classical.

As a Canadian cook and as a long-time admirer and friend of Craig's I'm excited to finally hold this book in my hands. It is an instant classic, a true record of what Canadian Cuisine at its best can be. Simple. Flavourful. Creative. And above all, firmly rooted in the soil of our farms, the clear water of our fisheries and the hearts of our cooks.

Thanks for the biscuits!

Chef Michael Smith

Introduction

As an apprentice chef, I worked and travelled widely throughout Europe in the mid-nineties, experiencing the highest level of contemporary creative cuisine as well as the classical French and European standards. At the same time, I also discovered a deep love of farming and centuries-old food-production techniques. I spent my time off in small villages, trying out local cheeses and sausages. I always felt that the craftsmanship and care that producers of these foods put into their work gave their dishes a unique character, because the ingredients originated in one geographic area.

Like many other cooks, I always dreamed of owning my own restaurant, and in 2001 I opened my bistro, Chives, in Halifax, Nova Scotia. The key to the success of Chives stems from my apprentice days: the understanding that fresh, locally grown, in-season ingredients taste better than those shipped in from far and wide. Whereas some restaurants have one main supplier, the "big white truck" of the restaurant world, we have nearly 100 that contribute to my menus throughout the year. My main role in the "prep" at Chives is to source ingredients, so I spend many days driving through the back roads of Nova Scotia seeking out farms, fishermen and cheese makers.

Quality of ingredients is the first, and possibly the most important, consideration for a cook, and I am often asked why fresh, locally produced fruits, vegetables, meats, fish and artisan food products like cheese, charcuterie meats and even wine are better. Food products that are shipped all over the world have usually been treated or picked under-ripe for transport. They are often mass-produced and full of hormones and pesticides. Purchasing produce in-season and from a smaller geographic range eliminates the need for preserving methods, allows easier quality control and ensures your food is harvested at the right time, when it is at its best.

The benefits to the environment are obvious as well. Millions of gallons of fuel are burned to ensure that Canadians are supplied with romaine lettuce and numerous other out-of-season food products in February. Even in the realm of "organics" — the big buzzword these days — large supermarket chains offer more and more organically produced foods from all over the world. It sounds healthy on one hand, but food products are still being trucked from ... who knows where? The paradox is obvious: we burn more and more fossil fuel to bring us "cleaner" food.

I have developed a deep respect for the people who produce the foods I use in my menus. The relationships I have nurtured since Chives opened have not only improved my cooking but have also had a great impact on me personally. I now grow some of my own food in a restaurant garden and orchard in the Annapolis Valley. Understanding the work behind food production of all types, the financial struggles of our farmers and how the food on our tables is taken for granted in our "have it all, have it now" society has made me a better person as well as a better chef. Bringing back an appreciation for our food producers has become a bit of a mission for me, and I try to demonstrate it the best way I know how ... on the plate. Fortunately, more and more people are adopting the idea that fresh and local produce is a great approach to cooking, and to dining. I hope that this book will offer you lots of new ideas about how to take advantage of this philosophy to produce great-tasting dishes.

All the recipes in this book have all been served at one time or another at Chives. They represent the very best from the past seven years, and each has been

adapted and then tested for the home kitchen. Within each chapter the recipes are categorized by season.

Almost every ingredient listed here is obtainable in season at farm markets or quality grocery stores across Canada. I encourage you to take the time to visit the markets in your area and choose only the best and freshest in-season local products you can find. This effort will pay off both in flavour and in your enjoyment of the process of cooking — the creation of memorable experiences for you, your family and your friends. If you're already a committed local market shopper, I hope you'll find many new ideas here for what you can do with the produce you find on display there.

I could not have taken the time needed to realize my dream of writing a cookbook without the support and hard work of the entire staff at Chives. Special thanks to Darren Lewis for his support of the project, for his help in testing and for the recipes he contributed from his own "little black book."

No single recipe in this book would be possible without the tireless efforts of the farmers and producers of Nova Scotia. The care and dedication they have for their craft makes the work of cooks like me easier.

Thank you to Bob and Janine Durning for their many hours in the kitchen testing recipes and for giving very useful feedback.

To all the chefs at the Culinary Institute of Canada, especially Hans Anderegg, thank you for teaching me about the wonderful history of classical food and how to build flavour in my cooking.

Thank you to the gang at Formac, especially Meghan Collins and Christen Thomas, for putting trust in my cooking and giving life to an idea. Thanks to Alanna Jankov for her creativity in the photography.

To my mentor, Michael Smith, thank you for your support and guidance over the years. It was in his kitchen at The Inn at Bay Fortune that I first learned how to think about food, to pick ingredients from a garden and to be a Canadian cook.

A special thank you to my Uncle John, whom I stood beside, stirring spaghetti sauce and clam chowder as a kid. He was the first true cook I ever knew.

And finally, thank you to my family: to my brother Jason for giving me a nudge on more than one occasion; to my father for always being there; and to my mother for nourishing body and soul.

Soups

Every one of us has a childhood memory of soup. Perhaps it was a bowl of chicken noodle when we were feeling under the weather, a bowl of beef and barley after a day of skating at the arena, or a bowl of hot turkey vegetable broth a few days after Thanksgiving. There is a long heritage and tradition in the soup kettles of Canada.

In many parts of Canada, certain types of soup have become classics, such as the ever-present chowder on the east coast. Maritimers know that there's much more to a good chowder than scraps of seafood tossed into a milky sauce: it requires the very best and freshest fish and shellfish, a smooth clean broth and just the right amount of velvety cream. Chowder-making has become a bit of a passion with me and I have presented some different styles here for you to try.

Compiling the soup recipes to include in this book was a harder task than for any other type of dish. I had endless ideas for soups but no actual recipes — often the starting point was only an onion, a stalk of celery and my imagination. And that's the way many excellent soups are created.

In the following pages you will find some simple soups and some that will impress discerning guests at your next dinner party. Each one, however, is distinctly Canadian, pays homage to our grandmothers' recipes and is seasonally inspired.

Fiddlehead Soup with Smoked-Gouda Cheese Soufflés

Fiddlehead ferns are the quintessential Maritime ingredient, but the season is short, especially when you are looking for perfect fiddleheads with tight spirals and few visible leaves. This soup is puréed and is an excellent way to enjoy fiddleheads a little later in the season when they are slightly overgrown. I often garnish the soup with a few sautéed fiddleheads and a cheese crisp, but it is not necessary. The soufflé is twice-baked so there is no need to worry about it collapsing before it reaches the table. It can be made the day before and reheated in the oven.

Soup

1 cup (250 mL) chopped onion
½ cup (125 mL) chopped celery
3 cloves garlic
3 stalks fresh thyme
1 tsp (5 mL) salt
1 tsp (5 mL) ground black pepper
2 tbsp (30 mL) olive oil
2 tbsp (30 mL) butter
½ cup (125 mL) white wine
5 cups (1.25 L) fiddleheads (washed well in cold water)
6 cups (1.5 L) chicken or vegetable stock
1 cup (250 mL) heavy cream (35% m.f.), optional
2 tsp (10 mL) lemon juice

Soufflés

½ cup (125 mL) unsalted butter
3/4 cup (180 mL) unbleached white flour
2 cups (500 mL) milk (2% m.f.)
¼ cup (60 mL) minced shallots
1 clove garlic, minced
1 tsp (5 mL) salt
1 tsp (5 mL) ground white pepper
⅛ tsp (1 mL) freshly grated nutmeg
5 free-range eggs, separated
1 cup (250 mL) grated smoked Gouda cheese
2 tbsp (30 mL) butter (second amount)
3 tbsp (45 mL) breadcrumbs

For the soup: Sauté onion, celery, garlic, thyme, salt and pepper in olive oil and butter over medium heat for 5 minutes. Deglaze the pan with white wine and bring to a boil. Add fiddleheads and stock and simmer for 20 minutes. Carefully purée in a blender. Strain soup into a clean saucepan and add cream and lemon juice.

For the cheese soufflés: Melt butter in a small saucepan over medium heat and add flour. Mix well until a crumbly paste forms. Set aside to cool.

In a second saucepan combine milk, shallots, garlic, salt, pepper and nutmeg and bring to a boil. Add to the cool roux in the first saucepan, stirring constantly. As the sauce thickens stir with a whisk to remove any lumps. Simmer over very low heat for 15 minutes. Refrigerate until cool.

Beat egg whites to stiff peaks. Add grated cheese and egg yolks to the cool sauce. Fold into this mixture the beaten egg whites. Grease 6 ramekins with butter and dust with breadcrumbs. Fill ramekins with mixture and bake in a preheated 375°F oven (190°C) for 15 minutes or until soufflés are golden brown. Allow to cool for 30 minutes, then remove from ramekins. Prior to serving, reheat soufflés in a 350°F (180°C) oven for 7 minutes. Sprinkle with additional cheese, if desired.

Ladle the soup into a heated shallow soup bowl and place a warmed soufflé in the centre of the bowl (see photograph). Garnish with sauteed fresh fiddleheads.

Serves 6, with some leftover soup for the next day

Smoked Yukon Gold Potato Chowder with Seared Arctic Char

This unique chowder base is fantastic with any seafood, but I have recently discovered incredible organic, farm-raised Arctic char in Nova Scotia that works particularly well. If you can't find Arctic char in your area, use wild salmon or farm-raised trout instead. If you do not want to go to the trouble of smoking the potatoes, use a tablespoon of liquid smoke, available at most grocery stores.

Soup
1 ½ lb (700 g) Yukon Gold potatoes, peeled and quartered
1 cup (250 mL) maple, apple or hickory wood chips
1 cup (250 mL) diced onion
½ cup (125 mL) chopped celery
1 cup (250 mL) sliced leek (white part only)
3 cloves garlic
2 tsp (10 mL) salt
2 tsp (10 mL) white pepper
¼ cup (60 mL) butter
½ cup (125 mL) white wine
6 cups (1.5 L) chicken broth
1 cup (250 mL) heavy cream (35% m.f.)

Seared Arctic Char
1 lb (450 g) Arctic char fillets, cut into 8 x 2-oz (60-g) pieces
3 tbsp (45 mL) olive oil
chives, for garnish
extra-virgin olive oil, for garnish

Using a barbecue or stove-top smoker, smoke potatoes over high heat for five minutes once the wood chips begin to smoke.

In a medium stockpot, sauté onion, celery, leeks, garlic, salt and pepper in butter until translucent. Deglaze the pot with white wine and reduce by half. Add potatoes, broth and cream and simmer for 90 minutes. Purée in a well-vented blender, strain into a clean saucepan and keep warm on a low burner.

Preheat a nonstick frying pan and sear char pieces in a little olive oil. Season with salt and pepper.

To serve, portion chowder into hot bowls and place 2 pieces of char in the centre of each bowl. Garnish with sliced chives and a drizzle of extra-virgin olive oil and, if you are adventurous, homemade potato chips.

Serves 4, with some leftover soup for the next day

Lobster and Halibut Chowder with Anise and Tarragon

This preparation is like a traditional Maritime chowder: it is milk-and-potato based and showcases some familiar and cherished spring seafood. Feel free to substitute any white fish or shellfish if you do not have halibut, but try not to miss the anise and tarragon. The scented ingredients work extremely well with lobster and add a comforting twist to the common chowder flavour profile.

¼ cup (60 mL) chopped shallots
1 cup (250 mL) chopped anise
½ cup (125 mL) chopped celery
1 clove garlic
1 tsp (5 mL) salt
½ tsp (2 mL) freshly ground white pepper
2 tbsp (30 mL) butter
3 cups (750 mL) peeled and diced potato
3 bay leaves
4 sprigs fresh tarragon (leaves removed, stalks reserved)
1 ½ to 2 lb (700 to 900 g) lobster, cooked and cleaned (shell reserved)
zest of ½ lemon
½ cup (125 mL) white wine
2 cups (500 mL) milk (2% m.f. or homogenized)
4 cups (1 L) chicken, fish or vegetable stock
1 cup (250 mL) heavy cream (35% m.f.)
1 fresh halibut fillet (8 oz/250 g)
2 tbsp (30 mL) extra-virgin olive oil

In a large saucepan, sauté shallots, anise, celery, garlic, salt and pepper in butter over medium heat for 5 minutes. Add potatoes, bay leaves, tarragon stalks, lobster shells and lemon zest. Deglaze the pan with white wine and bring to a boil. Add milk and stock, bring soup to a simmer and cook for 45 minutes.

Purée soup by carefully adding to a blender in small amounts. Leave the top vented but covered with a kitchen towel while blending to allow the steam to escape. Do not remove lobster shells, as they will give excellent flavour to the chowder (as in lobster bisque). Strain soup into a clean saucepan.

Cut halibut into pieces, bite-sized or one per person. The fresh lobster meat can be prepared much the same way, cut into small pieces, or served in larger pieces such as a claw or tail portion. Just prior to serving, add heavy cream, lobster meat and halibut pieces to the pan. Return pan to heat. Once the soup simmers the halibut will cook in about 90 seconds.

Serve immediately, garnished with chopped tarragon leaves and a drizzle of extra-virgin olive oil.

Serves 8 to 10

Sweet Pea and Basil Soup with Butter-Poached Lobster and Crème Fraiche

Many of the elements of this soup have a certain sweetness, so the tartness of the crème fraiche balances well. To butter-poach lobster properly, you will need raw lobster meat out of the shell. This can be purchased at most fish markets in the freezer section. It is quite expensive but for a "special-occasion soup" it is well worth the price. Fresh peas are essential for this recipe, and are usually available anywhere during peak season.

Soup
½ cup (125 mL) diced onion
¼ cup (60 mL) chopped celery
1 tbsp (15 mL) dried basil
1 tsp (5 mL) salt
1 tsp (5 mL) ground black pepper
3 tbsp (45 mL) extra-virgin olive oil
½ cup (125 mL) vermouth
3 cups (750 mL) freshly shelled peas
4 cups (1 L) vegetable stock
½ cup (125 mL) packed fresh basil
½ cup (125 mL) heavy cream (35% m.f.), optional

Poached lobster
½ lb (225 g) salted butter
1 tbsp (15 mL) water
2 raw lobster tails, shell removed
1 tsp (5 mL) fleur de sel

Crème fraiche
1 cup (250 mL) heavy cream (35% m.f.)
¼ cup (60 mL) buttermilk

For the soup: Sauté onion, celery, dried basil, salt and pepper in olive oil in a medium-sized saucepan, over medium heat for 10 minutes, until onion turns golden. Deglaze the pan with vermouth and reduce by half. Add peas and vegetable stock and bring to a simmer, cooking for 15 minutes. Purée in a blender with the top vented, and add fresh basil at the very end. Strain into a clean saucepan and reheat soup. Add heavy cream just before serving.

For the butter-poached lobster: Dice butter into approximately 20 pieces. Heat a small saucepan and add water. When water is warm, slowly add butter, piece by piece, whisking steadily. The butter will emulsify and foam slightly. When all the butter is incorporated add lobster tails and set pan on a burner at the "minimum" mark. Gently poach lobster for about 6 to 8 minutes. Never allow the butter to boil. Remove lobster from butter when it is firm to the touch, and slice into 4 portions. Season with a little fleur de sel just prior to serving.

For the crème fraiche: Mix cream and buttermilk in a bowl, cover in plastic film and set on a counter for 24 hours.

To serve, ladle about 6 oz (180 mL) of hot pea soup into a shallow bowl. Spoon a little crème fraiche in the centre and place lobster on top. Garnish with a leaf of fresh basil.

Serves 4 to 6, with some leftover soup for the next day

Field Tomato and Basil Soup with a Cherry Tomato Confit and Ricotta Crouton

Great cooks use texture as a way of making food fun to eat. Combining smooth soup with a crisp crouton and creamy ricotta cheese makes a seemingly common soup an exciting treat. This simple soup combines two classic flavours — tomato and basil — but the presentation and the sweetness of the confit of cherry tomatoes are most striking. This soup is also extremely healthy and has no added fat.

Soup

3 lb (1.3 kg) ripe field tomatoes (red or orange), roughly chopped
¼ cup (60 mL) chopped shallots
4 tbsp (60 mL) Roasted Garlic Purée (see recipe in "Basics")
1 tbsp (15 mL) dried basil
½ cup (125 mL) packed fresh basil leaves
2 cups (500 mL) tomato juice
2 cups (500 mL) chicken or vegetable stock
1 tsp (5 mL) salt
1 tsp (5 mL) freshly ground black pepper
1 tsp (5 mL) white sugar, optional

Confit and croutons

1 pint (500 mL) ripe cherry tomatoes
1 clove garlic
1 bay leaf
2 sprigs thyme
1 shallot, quartered
1 cup (250 mL) extra-virgin olive oil
1 cup (250 mL) creamy ricotta cheese
8 slices toasted baguette (cut diagonally)
small basil leaves, for garnish

For the soup: Combine all soup ingredients in a soup or small stockpot and simmer for 1 hour. Purée and adjust seasoning to taste. Some tomatoes are more acidic than others so a touch of sugar may be added if necessary.

For the confit: Peel the cherry tomatoes: use a small paring knife to cut an "X" on the bottom of each; blanch tomatoes for 10 seconds in boiling water and plunge *immediately* in iced water. The skins will now peel off easily.

In a small saucepan or loaf pan, place tomatoes, garlic, bay leaf, thyme and shallot. Add the olive oil and heat to 180°F (80°C), using a thermometer for accuracy. You will need enough olive oil to just cover the vegetables completely but 1 cup (250 mL) should do it. Place pan in a 150°F (65°C) oven for 3 hours, then allow to cool on the countertop.

To serve, spread or pipe ricotta cheese onto each slice of toasted baguette and garnish with tomato confit and a few small basil leaves or sliced chives. The tomato and ricotta crouton can be served on the side of the soup or resting on the edge of the bowl, as pictured. The olive oil from the cherry tomato confit can be used to garnish the soup just prior to serving.

Serves 8

Riesling-braised Leek and Chive Olive Oil Chowder with Pan-fried Mackerel and Tempura Oysters

Mackerel is an under-utilized fish in the culinary world, although most Maritimers grow up eating it with garden potatoes and chow chow. Larger fish can be fatty but smaller ones have just the right amount of buttery smoothness for this delicious recipe.

Chowder
3 cups (750 mL) sliced leek (in ¼ inch/5 mm rings), white part only
2 tbsp (30 mL) butter
2 cups (500 mL) Riesling wine
3 cups (750 mL) peeled and diced new potatoes
2 shallots, coarsely chopped
2 cloves garlic
¾ cup (180 mL) chopped celery
¾ cup (180 mL) chopped anise
6 cups (1500 mL) chicken broth
1 tsp (5 mL) sea salt
1 tsp (5 mL) freshly ground black pepper
1 cup (250 mL) heavy cream (35% m.f.)
2 cups (500 mL) canola oil
4 mackerel fillets, about 4 oz (100 g) each, cut into 2-oz (50-g) pieces
3 tbsp (45 mL) olive oil
16 medium choice oysters, shucked, with oyster liquor reserved
1 ½ cups (375 mL) Simple Tempura Batter (recipe follows)
3 tbsp (45 mL) Chive Olive Oil (see recipe in "Basics")

Simple tempura batter
1 egg yolk
½ cup (125 mL) iced water
1 tbsp (15 mL) white wine
⅛ tsp (0.5 mL) baking powder
⅛ tsp (0.5 mL) salt
½ cup (125 mL) white flour

For the chowder: Sauté leeks in butter for 2 minutes and add Riesling. Cover the pot and braise for 30 minutes on low heat.

In a soup pot, place potatoes, shallots, garlic, celery, anise, chicken broth, salt and pepper and bring to a boil. Cook until potatoes are tender. Purée soup in a blender, pass through a fine-meshed chinois or strainer and place in a clean pot over low heat. Add cream and leeks, including any wine remaining from the braising procedure. Also add the reserved oyster liquor. Allow soup to simmer on very low heat until you are ready to serve.

For the mackerel and oysters: It is important to cook the mackerel and oysters at the same time, just prior to serving. This will keep the oysters crispy and the mackerel hot and perfectly cooked. Heat a non-stick frying pan to medium high and add the olive oil. At the same time, in a steep-sided saucepan, heat canola oil to 350°F (180°C). The oil should be about 2 inches (5 cm) deep, so add a little more if necessary. Season each mackerel fillet with a little salt and pepper and sauté in the nonstick pan for 2 minutes on each side. While the fish is cooking, dip oysters in tempura batter and fry in 2 batches (8 at a time) in canola oil. Remove oysters with a slotted spoon and rest on a clean paper towel. Season with a small amount of salt and pepper as soon as oysters are removed from the oil.

For the tempura batter: Mix egg yolk, water and wine well. Add dry ingredients and whisk together very quickly until smooth. Use immediately.

Yields 1 cup (250 mL)

To serve, ladle 6 oz (180 mL) of chowder into a bowl and set 2 pieces of seared mackerel in the middle. Rest 2 oyster fritters on top of the mackerel — not in the soup — to prevent the tempura from becoming wet. Garnish with a teaspoon of chive olive oil drizzled around the soup.

Serves 8

Corn "Off the Cob" Soup with Smokehaus Bacon, Chipotle Cream and Browned-Butter Cornbread

This soup takes a little work but it will convert any corn-chowder lovers. The intensity of the corn flavour is heightened by using the cobs to make the broth and by using cornmeal instead of a roux to thicken the soup. Essentially this is a very, very loose Italian polenta. Milk gives the soup a corn chowder essence, but for those with lactose concerns it works equally well without. In early autumn fresh, locally-grown corn is available almost everywhere.

Soup
6 cobs of corn (kernels removed, cobs reserved)
2 cups (500 mL) milk (2% m.f. or homogenized)
6 cups (1.5 L) low-sodium chicken broth
½ cup (125 mL) finely sliced double-smoked bacon
1 cup (250 mL) minced onion
3 cloves garlic, minced
½ cup (125 mL) minced celery
1 tsp (5 mL) dried sage or summer savory
1 tbsp (15 mL) salt
1 tbsp (15 mL) ground black pepper
4 tbsp (60 mL) butter
½ cup (125 mL) sherry
⅓ cup (75 mL) cornmeal
1 tsp (5 mL) hot sauce
1 tbsp (15 mL) chopped sage
1 tbsp (15 mL) chopped chives
½ cup (125 mL) heavy cream (35% m.f.)

Chipotle cream
3 dried chipotle peppers
1 cup (250 mL) water
½ cup (125 mL) sour cream
4 tbsp (60 mL) heavy cream (35% m.f.)

Cornbread
1 ½ (375 mL) cups coarse yellow cornmeal
1 cup (250 mL) fine white cornmeal
1 cup (250 mL) unbleached white flour
2 tsp (10 mL) sea salt
1 tbsp (15 mL) baking powder
½ tsp (2 mL) paprika
¼ tsp (1 mL) cayenne pepper
¾ cup (180 mL) whole milk
1 ¼ cups (325 mL) buttermilk
2 large free-range eggs
4 tbsp (60 mL) melted unsalted butter plus 1 tbsp (15 mL) cold butter

For the soup: In a stockpot, cover cleaned corn cobs with milk and chicken broth. Simmer for 30 minutes. Discard cobs and set cob broth aside.

In a large-diameter saucepan, gently fry sliced bacon until golden brown. Add corn kernels, onion, garlic, celery, sage, salt, pepper and butter and sauté over medium heat until onions and kernels of corn caramelize slightly. This will take about 15 minutes. Deglaze the pan with sherry. Add cob broth and bring to a boil. Add cornmeal in a steady stream, stirring constantly. Simmer for 1 hour on low heat to soften cornmeal and thicken the soup. Add hot sauce, fresh herbs, and cream just prior to serving.

For the chipotle cream: Soak peppers in water until they soften, about an hour. In a food processor, add hydrated peppers to sour cream and purée until smooth. If possible, store the sauce in a squeeze or used mustard bottle.

To serve, ladle the soup into a soup bowl and use the chipotle squeeze to garnish the soup. Place a piece of cornbread in the centre of the bowl and garnish with chives.

For the cornbread: In a mixing bowl combine all dry ingredients and mix well. In a second bowl whisk together eggs, milk, buttermilk and melted butter. Combine to form a batter. Pour into a preheated and oiled baking dish or, ideally, a cast-iron pan. Bake at 400° F for 15 to 20 minutes or until golden brown. Rub the top of the cornbread with the pat of cold butter.

Serves 10 to 12

Intense Carrot and Ginger Soup

I call this soup "intense" on my menus because I love the taste of ginger and do not shy away from using plenty in this recipe. I rely heavily on my professional-series blender for any puréed soup, but you can do a great job simply by turning your blender on and leaving it for 2 minutes. Straining any puréed soup through a fine-meshed chinois will make it super-creamy on the palate.

6 cups (1.5 L) peeled and roughly chopped carrots
1 cup (250 mL) diced onion
2 cloves garlic
1 cup (250 mL) chopped celery
½ cup (125 mL) extra-virgin olive oil
1 tbsp (15 mL) ground black pepper
2 tbsp (30 mL) salt
2 tbsp (30 mL) dried ginger
6 cups (1.5 L) chicken broth
1 cup (250 mL) freshly squeezed orange juice
½ cup (125 mL) coarsely chopped fresh ginger
1 cup (250 mL) heavy cream (35% m.f.)

Preheat oven to 400°F (200°C).

In a mixing bowl, combine carrots, onion, garlic, celery, olive oil, pepper, salt and dried ginger. Mix well and spread vegetables on a baking sheet in a single layer. Roast in oven until golden brown (about 25 to 30 minutes).

In a soup or stockpot, combine vegetables, broth, orange juice, cream and fresh ginger.

Simmer soup for at least 1 hour. Purée well and strain through a fine-meshed chinois. You may need to adjust the liquid in the recipe as some water will evaporate during the simmering process. Just add a touch of water, stock or orange juice to achieve the desired consistency.

Serves 12

Italian Peasant Soup with Berkshire Pork Sausage and Fire-Roasted Tomatoes

This recipe from my co-chef at Chives, Darren Lewis, is one that benefits from using canned tomatoes. The other great ingredient in this soup is the Berkshire pork sausage, made by hand in the Annapolis Valley. This heirloom variety of free-range pork is growing in popularity and has a dark, moist flesh and better marbling than common pork loin, but you can use any good quality sausage. Choose one with a touch of spice, like chorizo or hot Italian.

6 hot Italian heritage pork sausages
2 cups (500 mL) diced onion
1 ½ cups (375 mL) diced celery
⅓ cup (75 mL) minced garlic
1 tbsp (15 mL) salt
1 tbsp (15 mL) ground black pepper
2 tbsp (30 mL) dried basil
½ cup (125 mL) olive oil
4 large Yukon gold potatoes, peeled and diced
1 small winter cabbage, shredded
2 cans white beans (8 oz/250 mL each)
2 cans fire-roasted tomatoes (8 oz/250 mL each)
10 cups (2.5 L) low-sodium chicken broth
2 cups (500 mL) heavy cream (35% m.f.)

Grill or bake sausages completely over medium heat to ensure they cook through without blackening the outside. Fresh sausages will take about 10 minutes. Allow to cool and slice on a slight bias about ¼ inch (5mm) thick. Sauté onion, celery, garlic, salt, pepper and basil in olive oil until onions are translucent. Add potatoes, shredded cabbage, white beans, tomatoes and chicken broth and bring to a simmer. When potatoes are tender add cream and serve.

Garnish soup with some simple croutons and grated Parmesan cheese if desired.

Serves 12

Salads

If you like to use local produce, making salads seasonally can often be a challenge in Canada. Although large grocery chains carry leafy greens year-round, I try to use the fantastic greenhouse greens from my own province. But salads do not have to have leafy greens to be interesting. I have moved beyond serving salads of the basic "tossed" variety into making vegetables the showcased ingredients.

Salads have a way of stripping down flavours to their basics, and I did not appreciate the difficulty of making a good salad until I had been cooking for a number of years. When building a salad now I look for certain criteria. First of all, everything must be absolutely fresh and "ready to use." By this I mean that tomatoes must be ripe, celery crisp, greens standing to attention, herbs fragrant and sweet — and so on. Finding textures that complement each other is the next step. Crunch is absolutely essential. If you are not using crisp greens, adding properly toasted nuts, orchard fruit or croutons can add a lot to your enjoyment of the dish.

If you want to make your salad into a complete meal, adding proteins like poached or grilled seafood, proscuitto, pancetta, sausages, cold beef or chicken or beans and lentils can transform a side dish into something bigger and better.

In this chapter you will find easy-to-make seasonal salads that can add nutrition to a family dinner, complement a barbecued steak or stand all on their own with a glass of Pinot Grigio.

Baby Spinach Salad with Maple-spiced Pecans, Goat's Cheese, Pickled Red Onions and Honey Buttermilk Dressing

Fresh leafy salads are often difficult early in the year — summer is the time of year when salads really shine — but this salad makes use of typical spring ingredients such as fresh spinach and maple syrup. It also uses items from the pantry like pickled red onions, nuts and honey. A hint on the dressing: season it very well. The spinach will water down the flavour of the creamy dressing if you go too light on the salt, pepper and hot sauce.

Salad
1 lb (450 g) fresh baby spinach leaves
½ cup (125 mL) Pickled Red Onions (see recipe in "Pickles and Preserves")
½ cup (125 mL) Honey Buttermilk Dressing (recipe follows)
1 cup (250 mL) Maple Spiced Pecans (recipe follows)
½ cup (125 mL) crumbled fresh goat's cheese

Honey buttermilk dressing
¼ cup (60 mL) apple cider vinegar
¼ cup (60 mL) natural organic sour cream
¼ cup (60 mL) buttermilk
1 tsp (5 mL) Dijon mustard
⅓ cup (80 mL) honey
1 clove garlic, minced
½ shallot, minced
1 tsp (5 mL) salt
1 tsp (5 mL) freshly ground black pepper
½ tsp (3 mL) Tabasco or similar hot sauce
2 tbsp (30 mL) chopped fresh chives
½ cup (125 mL) canola or pomace (light olive) oil

Maple spiced pecans
⅔ cup (160 mL) maple syrup
1 tbsp (15 mL) dried ginger
1 tbsp (15 mL) cinnamon
1 tbsp (15 mL) allspice
1 tsp (5 mL) cayenne pepper
1 tbsp (15 mL) salt
1 tsp (5 mL) ground black pepper
2 lb (1 kg) pecan halves

For the salad: To assemble the salad, toss greens with Pickled Red Onions and Honey Buttermilk Dressing. Divide into 4 or 6 bowls, depending on the desired portion size. Sprinkle with crumbled goat's cheese and 6 to 8 pecans per person.

Serves 4 to 6

For the dressing: In a mixing bowl or food processor, combine all ingredients except oil. Slowly add oil in a steady stream, whisking continuously. Store in a sealed jar in the refrigerator for up to 2 weeks.

Yields 2 cups (500 mL)

For the pecans: In a bowl, whisk maple syrup and spices together to combine. Add nuts and toss to coat well. Bake in a 275°F (135°C) oven until crisp, about 30 minutes. Stir nuts every 10 minutes during baking. Allow to cool completely and store in an airtight container. Do not refrigerate or the nuts will go soggy.

Darren's Caesar Salad with German Speck and Padano Curls

I once swore that I would never serve a Caesar salad at my restaurant. But I must confess that this is an excellent way to enjoy the familiar flavours of the classic Caesar. Before puréeing the garlic, slice each clove in half and remove the germ in the middle with the tip of a knife. This is where much of the peppery bitterness comes from and, since this garlic is not cooked, it will leave an unpleasant aftertaste in the dressing.

Salad
2 small heads young romaine lettuce
8 slices German speck or double-smoked bacon
1 crusty baguette
¼ cup (60 mL) extra-virgin olive oil
1 clove organic garlic
1 cup (250 mL) Caesar Dressing (recipe follows)
1 small chunk Grana Padano cheese
1 tbsp (15 mL) freshly squeezed lemon juice
2 tbsp (30 mL) extra-virgin olive oil (second amount)

Classic caesar dressing
1 oz (30 g) whole organic garlic cloves
1 oz (30 g) capers
1 oz (30 g) anchovies
¼ cup (60 mL) freshly squeezed lemon juice
zest of 1/2 lemon
3 egg yolks
1 tsp (5 mL) Tabasco sauce
1 tsp (5 mL) Worcestershire sauce
1 tsp (5 mL) salt
1 tsp (5 mL) freshly ground black pepper
2 ¼ cups (560 mL) light olive oil or pomace
⅓ cup (75 mL) grated Parmesan cheese

For the salad: Pick whole lettuce leaves apart and rinse under cold water. Pat dry with clean paper towels.

Sauté speck or bacon until crisp and allow to cool. Break into bite-sized pieces using your fingers and set aside.

To make garlic crostini, slice baguette 1 inch (2.5 cm) thick on the bias and brush with olive oil. Grill on the barbecue until crisp and toasted. Rub raw garlic clove along the length of the toasted bread 2 or 3 times.

Toss leaves of whole romaine in the Caesar dressing. Place in a single layer on a large platter and sprinkle with speck bits. Run a peeler along the length of the Padano cheese and allow curls of cheese to fall over the salad. Mix lemon juice and olive oil together and drizzle over the salad. Serve with grilled garlic crostini.

Serves 6

For the dressing: In a food processor, combine garlic, capers, anchovies, lemon juice, zest, egg yolks, Tabasco sauce, Worcestershire sauce, salt and pepper. Purée until homogenous but still with visible little pieces of capers and anchovies. Slowly add oil in a steady stream until it is all incorporated and dressing is smooth. Fold in Parmesan cheese and adjust seasoning if necessary to suit your personal taste. For a spicier sauce increase Tabasco and for a tangier sauce add extra lemon juice.

Yields 3 cups (750 mL)

Heirloom Tomato Salad with Bocconcini, Basil, Aged Balsamic Vinegar and Olive Oil

This is undoubtedly my favourite salad. Heirloom tomatoes are locally produced, non-hybrid varieties that have not been commercially produced in large quantities. Using beautiful heirloom tomatoes in this salad adds tremendous colour and a sweetness that you do not get with most mass-produced tomatoes. This salad is inspired by the traditional Insalate Caprese of Italy.

2 lb (1 kg) heirloom tomatoes (mixed varieties)
3 x 2-oz (60-g) balls fresh bocconcini (fresh baby mozzarella)
30 leaves fresh basil
2 tbsp (30 mL) chopped chives
6 tbsp (90 mL) aged balsamic vinegar (minimum 10-year)
½ cup (60 mL) extra-virgin olive oil
2 tbsp (30 mL) fleur de sel
several grindings of fresh black pepper

Slice, quarter or halve the different tomato varieties. This will add texture and visual appeal. On 6 small plates assemble tomatoes. Tear bocconcini cheese into small pieces and set on tomatoes, 1 oz (30 g) per plate. Add fresh basil leaves, about 5 per plate. Garnish each salad with a sprinkle of chopped chives, 1 tablespoon balsamic vinegar and 2 tablespoons olive oil, and season with fleur de sel and fresh pepper.

Serves 6

Grilled Summer Vegetable Salad with Mountain Ash Goat Cheese

On hot summer days this is the perfect accompaniment to a simple piece of grilled fish or even a great steak. It can be served hot if you are grilling at the last minute or served cold if you are preparing it the day before and taking it to a barbecue get-together. Mountain Ash goat cheese is a product unique to Nova Scotia but you can use any good-quality aged goat cheese, even feta. For a dressing I often drizzle olive oil and a good-quality sherry vinegar over the top, but Poached Garlic Vinaigrette works very well here.

12 button mushrooms, cleaned and whole
1 small red onion, quartered
2 green zucchini, sliced
12 pattypan squash, halved
1 small eggplant, sliced
3 ripe tomatoes
2 tbsp (30 mL) salt
1 tbsp (15 mL) pepper
1 tbsp (15 mL) dried basil
1 tbsp (15 mL) dried oregano
1 cup (250 mL) extra-virgin olive oil
12 cherry tomatoes
2 cups (500 mL) fresh arugula leaves
¼ cup (60 mL) sherry vinegar
12 oz (380 g) aged goat cheese

Preheat barbecue or stovetop grill on high and clean the rack very well.

In a large mixing bowl, toss mushrooms, onion, zucchini, squash, eggplant, ripe tomatoes, salt, pepper, basil and oregano in half the olive oil. Grill vegetables for a couple of minutes on each side or until they take colour. Arrange grilled vegetables on a platter or serving board and garnish with cherry tomatoes and arugula leaves. Drizzle sherry vinegar and remaining olive oil over the top, or use ½ cup of Poached-garlic Vinaigrette (see recipe pg. 58). Slice or shave goat cheese over salad.

Serves 6 to 8

Smoked Mackerel, Anise, Lemon and Honey Apple Salad

This salad was originally conceived as a garnish for poached salmon, but the unique flavours are so interesting that I now let the elements shine all on their own. Smoked mackerel is smooth and moist, due to the fat content of the fish. The honeycrisp apple, with its subtle sweetness and elegant snap, balances very well with the smoke and tangy lemon.

2 cups (500 mL) flaked smoked mackerel
½ anise bulb
2 honeycrisp apples, cut into matchsticks (julienned)
2 green onions (green tops only)
juice of 2 lemons
zest of 1 lemon
1 tsp (5 mL) Dijon mustard
1 tsp (5 mL) salt
½ tsp (3 mL) Tabasco sauce
6 tbsp (90 mL) extra-virgin olive oil
1 head Boston bibb lettuce

Carefully remove bones before flaking smoked mackerel. Shave anise as thinly as possible, using the large blade side of a hand grater (or ideally use a mandoline). Combine mackerel, anise, julienned apples and sliced green onion tops in a mixing bowl. In a separate bowl, combine lemon juice, zest, mustard, salt, Tabasco and olive oil and whisk to a smooth dressing. Toss salad elements with dressing and allow to rest in the refrigerator for 1 hour.

To serve salad, place 2 or 3 leaves of lettuce in the centre of a plate. Divide tossed salad into 4 equal portions over the lettuce.

Serves 4

My Ma's Broccoli Salad

Many versions of this classic salad can be found in delis, supermarkets and maybe in your mother's recipe file. This one is very, very good and I can honestly say that I cannot make this as well as my mother.

Salad

6 strips bacon
2 heads broccoli, cut into florets
¼ red onion, thinly sliced
1 cup (250 mL) grated old orange cheddar
½ cup (125 mL) raisins
1 small tin mandarin oranges, drained
Curried Mayo Dressing (recipe follows)
¼ cup (60 mL) almonds or pecan halves, optional

Curried mayo dressing

1 cup (250 mL) mayonnaise
⅓ cup (80 mL) white granulated sugar
2 tbsp (30 mL) red wine vinegar
½ tsp (3 mL) salt
1 tsp (5 mL) ground black pepper
2 cloves garlic, minced
1 tsp (5 mL) curry powder

For the salad: Cut bacon into ⅓-inch (1-cm) pieces and crisp in a frying pan. Drain off excess fat and place bacon on a paper towel to cool. In a large mixing bowl, combine broccoli, onion, cheese, raisins, orange segments and Curried Mayo Dressing and mix well. Let rest for several hours before serving so flavours can meld. Place in a large serving bowl and garnish with almonds, pecans or other nuts of your choice.

Serves 8 to 10

For the dressing: Combine all ingredients and mix until smooth.

Yields 1 ½ cups (375 mL)

"Opening Night" Salad (Greenhouse Lettuce, Apple, Blue Cheese, Smoked Almonds and Orange Shallot Vinaigrette)

I opened my restaurant on December 4, 2001, in Halifax, Nova Scotia. Finding a refreshing salad for the opening night menu was a challenge at that time of year. Fortunately, hydroponic lettuces are a great way to eat fresh greens throughout the year. Use a mesclun mix, Boston bibb or red leaf lettuce but avoid romaine or iceberg varieties for this particular salad — the dressing is tart and refreshing and does not benefit from watery lettuces.

Salad

1 head (approximately 8 to 10 oz/230 to 280 g) greenhouse lettuce, cleaned and dried
1 apple (any crisp variety), julienned into "matchsticks"
⅓ cup (80 mL) crumbled blue cheese
⅓ cup (80 mL) smoked almonds
4 oz (125 mL) Orange Shallot Vinaigrette (recipe follows)

Orange shallot vinaigrette

4 cups (1 L) fresh orange juice (not from concentrate)
zest of 1 orange
½ cup (125 mL minced) shallots
1 clove garlic, minced
1 tbsp (15 mL) Dijon mustard
¼ cup (60 mL) honey vinegar
1 tbsp (15 mL) salt
2 tsp (10 mL) pepper
2 cups (500 mL) light olive oil

For salad: Toss all ingredients together in a salad bowl and serve immediately.

Serves 4

For vinaigrette: In a saucepan, combine orange juice, zest, shallots and garlic and bring to a boil. Reduce liquid to ¼ of the original volume (about 1 cup/250 mL remaining). Remove from heat and allow to cool completely. Add mustard, vinegar, salt and pepper. Slowly add olive oil in a steady stream, whisking continuously. Store vinaigrette in a refrigerator for up to 3 weeks.

Yields 3 ½ cups (875 mL)

Appetizers

When I enter a restaurant, particularly one with a trusted chef, I am anxious to see what is being offered to whet my appetite.

Main-course dishes tend to be built following the template of a protein, a starch, a vegetable and a sauce, but appetizers or "starters" represent endless creative possibilities for the cook. Any ingredient can play a lead, the flavours are stripped down and simplicity and technique become most important. Because portion sizes are smaller, we tend to worry less about balancing multiple elements than we do with a main dish. With appetizers, cooks are not confined to any rules. Traditional dishes can be honoured yet re-invented to show a new and evolved style of Canadian cooking.

A bowl of freshly steamed mussels with drawn butter, a sea scallop with sauce Marie Rose, a flaky biscuit with maple butter, an oyster on the half shell, a leg of crisped duck confit or a plate of perfectly grilled asparagus — all are dishes that can inspire the palate and create excitement for the meal ahead.

Appetizers are rarely intended to stand alone as the centerpiece of the meal, but any one of the recipes presented here can be enjoyed either as a precursor to a grand meal, or as a light lunch. Some can even be served as a main course with a few additions and a little creativity on your part.

Asparagus and Smoked-Oyster Crumpets

The ultimate spring vegetable, asparagus grows wild in Nova Scotia and other parts of Canada, but it is primarily cultivated. Tender new asparagus does not need peeling, but sometimes using a peeler on the bottom 2 inches (5 cm) improves the tenderness if you are simply serving them steamed. Adding oysters cultivated in Nova Scotia, PEI or British Columbia to the dish showcases the spring jewels of field and sea.

Crumpets
1 cup (250 mL) unbleached white flour
1 ½ tsp (8 mL) white sugar
¼ tsp (2 mL) salt
1 ½ tbsp (8 mL) baking powder
1 egg plus 1 egg yolk
¼ cup (125 mL) milk
½ cup (60 mL) clarified unsalted butter

Asparagus and oysters
18 choice oysters, shucked, liquor reserved
1 cup (250 mL) apple wood chips, soaked in water
1 shallot, minced
1 clove garlic, minced
1 ¼ tsp (6 mL) salt
½ tsp (3 mL) pepper
4 tbsp (60 mL) butter
2 tbsp (30 mL) flour
2 oz (60 mL) dry vermouth or white wine
¼ cup (60 mL) rich chicken broth
¾ cup (180 mL) heavy cream (35% m.f.)
3 tbsp (45 mL) chopped chives
1 lb (454 g) bunch of asparagus
2 tbsp (30 mL) water

For the crumpets: Thoroughly mix all dry ingredients in a bowl. In a separate small bowl, beat eggs and milk. Add egg mixture to flour and stir to combine. Add 2 tablespoons (30 mL) of melted butter. The batter should have the consistency of a very thick pancake mix.

In a nonstick skillet, heat 3 tablespoons of clarified butter over medium heat. Drop a ¼-cup (60 mL) measure of the batter in the pan and cook until crisp and golden brown in colour. Flip crumpet only when bubbles appear on the top. It may be necessary to add a few more drops of butter to the pan when the crumpet is flipped. This recipe yields 8 to 10 crumpets.

For the asparagus and oysters: Lightly smoke raw oysters on a grill or resting rack over applewood chips on a barbecue or in a covered roasting pan on the stovetop. The oysters will turn opaque after about 5 minutes. Remove from heat and allow to cool.

In a small saucepan, sauté shallot, garlic, 1 tsp (5 mL) salt and pepper in 2 tbsp (30 mL) of butter for 3 or 4 minutes over medium heat. Do not allow onions and garlic to brown. Add flour and stir to form a roux. Add vermouth, then chicken broth, stirring continuously. The sauce will begin to thicken. Add cream and reserved oyster liquor. Bring to a boil. Reduce heat and simmer sauce for 15 minutes, then strain through a fine-meshed chinois. Add smoked oysters and chopped chives and bring back to a simmer. The oysters will cook in 2 minutes.

Sauté cleaned asparagus in remaining butter with 2 tbsp of water. Season with ¼ tsp (2 mL) salt and a touch of freshly ground pepper.

To serve, heat crumpets in a toaster or oven for a couple of minutes until warm. Place sautéed asparagus on top, then three oysters per person. Drizzle a little of the sauce over the top and garnish with a few more chopped chives if desired.

Serves 6

Grilled Asparagus with Tomato Vinaigrette

This is another great vegetable side dish that works as well chilled as it does warm. As a salad, it goes well with cold meats and cheese, crusty French bread and a cold Pinot Grigio. Served just off the grill it is perfect with barbecued salmon or pork chops. The vinaigrette is a great "go to" recipe as you can use jarred or dried sun-dried tomatoes from your pantry. I buy my local asparagus each year at the Halifax Farmer's Market, but during the season supermarket chains have been doing a better job featuring locally grown at a reasonable price.

Asparagus
2 lbs (1 kg) asparagus
3 tbsp (45 mL) extra-virgin olive oil
½ tsp (3 mL) salt
½ tsp (3 mL) pepper
½ cup (125 mL) Tomato Vinaigrette (recipe follows)
fresh basil leaves, for garnish

Tomato vinaigrette
½ cup (125 mL) sun-dried tomatoes
1 shallot, minced
1 clove garlic, minced
½ cup (125 mL) white balsamic vinegar
½ tsp (3 mL) dried basil
½ tsp (3 mL) salt
1 tsp (5 mL) white sugar
1 tsp (5 mL) Tabasco or other hot sauce
1 cup (250 mL) extra-virgin olive oil

For the asparagus: Preheat stovetop grill or barbecue on high. Clean the surface very well with an iron brush and/or old rag. Clean asparagus and remove woody bottoms of the stems, then toss them in olive oil, salt and pepper. It is important that the asparagus is kissed with the oil but not drowning in it, as that will cause flare-ups. Grill asparagus for about 5 to 6 minutes, turning constantly while grilling.

To serve, set asparagus on a platter with all the pointed, flowering ends aligned in the same direction. Drizzle with 6 oz (180 mL) of Tomato Vinaigrette and garnish with fresh basil leaves.

Serves 4 to 6

For the vinaigrette: Soak tomatoes in water to soften if necessary. Most jarred tomatoes are packed in oil and will be soft enough already. Drain any excess oil (for added flavour reserve some of the tomato oil to use instead of olive oil).

Pulse tomatoes in a food processor. Add shallot, garlic, vinegar, basil, salt, sugar and hot sauce and purée on high until smooth. Slowly add olive oil in a steady stream until vinaigrette emulsifies. Store in a sealed jar in the refrigerator for up to a month.

Yields 1 ½ cups (375 mL)

Lobster à la King with Sweet Peas

The very best way to enjoy this dish is to use lobster stock or lobster bisque as the base for the cream sauce, but a rich chicken stock makes a good substitute. Whether you call this dish Lobster à la King or Lobster Bruschetta, the outcome is the same — luxurious comfort food. Many small local bakeries make baguettes daily, and the bread should be used on the day of purchase.

Lobster à la king

1 shallot, minced
1 cup (250 mL) shelled sweet peas
1 tsp (5 mL) salt
1 tsp (5 mL) pepper
1 tbsp (15 mL) butter
3 tbsp (45 mL) dry sherry
1 cup (250 mL) Lobster Bisque (recipe follows)
¼ cup (60 mL) heavy cream (35% m.f.)
2 cups (500 mL) chopped cooked lobster meat (reserved from bisque recipe below)
2 tbsp (30 mL) chopped fresh tarragon
2 tbsp (30 mL) chopped fresh chives
¼ cup (60 mL) grated Parmesan cheese
6 slices toasted baguette

Lobster bisque

2 x 1 ½-lb (675-g) lobsters
2 tbsp (30 mL) olive oil
2 tbsp (30 mL) butter
2 medium onions (or 1 large), coarsely chopped
1 stalks celery, coarsely chopped
2 medium-sized carrots, coarsely chopped
4 cloves garlic
1 cup (250 mL) diced tomatoes (or 1 small can)
3 bay leaves
3 sprigs fresh thyme
4 tbsp (60 mL) flour
1 cup (250 mL) sherry
3 cups (750 mL) chicken broth
1 cup (250 mL) calm juice (or 1 small jar)
½ cup (125 mL) tomato paste (or 1 small tin)
1 cup (250 mL) heavy cream (35% m.f.)
salt and pepper to taste

For the Lobster à la King: In a saucepan, sauté shallots, peas, salt and pepper in the butter for 3 minutes. Add sherry and reduce until the pan is dry. Add bisque and cream and bring to a boil. Add lobster meat, fresh herbs and Parmesan cheese and just warm lobster meat through. Spoon lobster and cream mixture over toasted baguette and serve immediately.

Serves 6

For the bisque: Cook lobsters for 8 to 10 minutes in just enough boiling water to cover them. Remove lobsters and reserve cooking liquid. Chill lobsters, then remove meat from shells. Roughly chop lobster shells into manageable pieces and refrigerate meat in a sealed container for later use.

Heat a stockpot and sauté lobster shells in olive oil for 10 minutes or until they begin to brown slightly. Add butter, onions, celery, carrots, garlic, tomatoes, bay leaves and thyme and cook for 10 more minutes on medium heat. Add flour to make a roux and deglaze the pan with sherry. Add chicken broth and 3 cups of reserved lobster cooking liquid along with the clam juice and tomato paste. Bring to a boil and simmer for 1 hour, reducing overall volume by half. Strain bisque through a chinois or strainer, pressing firmly on shells and vegetables to extract all the liquid. Place strained soup back on the heat and add cream. Bring back to a boil and adjust seasoning with salt and pepper. Any leftover bisque can be frozen and served alone as a soup later.

Yields 3 litres

Fish 'n' Chips (Fried Cod Cheeks with Fingerling Potato Crisps and Anise Slaw)

Fish 'n' chips is easily the most common restaurant menu item in the Maritimes, if not all of Canada. This is a fun version that you can try at home. Try pairing it with Bread & Butter pickles. The use of preserves is a huge tradition in Canadian cooking. Despite my constant quest to find the best fresh ingredients, I still love cracking open a jar of pickles, jam, jelly or chutney from the previous year. It's like putting culinary history on your plate.

Fish 'n' chips

1 lb (450 g) fresh cod cheeks
½ cup (125 mL) flour
3 tsp (15 mL) salt
1 tsp (5 mL) pepper
2 eggs
3 tbsp (45 mL) milk
1 cup (250 mL) panko (Japanese breadcrumbs)
10 fingerling potatoes, about 3 in (7.5 cm) long
8 cups (2 L) canola oil

Coleslaw

1 bulb anise, thinly sliced
¼ cup (60 mL) julienned red pepper
juice and zest of 1 lemon
2 tbsp (30 mL) chopped anise fronds
4 tbsp (60 mL) extra-virgin olive oil
¼ tsp (1 mL) salt
¼ tsp (1 mL) pepper

For the fish 'n' chips: Each cod cheek has a small muscle and membrane on its side that can be removed easily with your fingers. Pat cheeks dry using some paper towel. To bread the cod you will require three bowls. In the first bowl, mix flour, 1 tsp (5 mL) salt and the pepper. In the second bowl mix eggs and milk, and in the third bowl place breadcrumbs. Dredge cod cheeks in flour, then in egg, and finally in breadcrumbs. Set aside on a clean plate.

Slice fingerling potatoes on a mandoline as thinly as you can (about 1/16 in/1 mm thick). Rinse in cold water then dry as much as possible on paper towels.

Use a steep-sided pot with a wide mouth for deep-frying. The oil should go no more than 1/3 of the way up the sides. Heat the canola oil to 300 °F (150°C), using a deep-fry thermometer. Begin with the potatoes as you will serve these cold like potato chips. Carefully drop them in the fat and fry until lightly golden. Remove from heat and place in a bowl lined with paper towel. Season with the remaining salt.

Increase the heat of the oil until the thermometer reads 360°F (185°C). Fry cod cheeks until they float and are a deep golden brown.

For the coleslaw: Mix all ingredients in a bowl and refrigerate overnight.

Serves 4 to 6

Chanterelle Mushroom Strudel with Spinach Sauce and Greek Yogurt

Foraging for chanterelle mushrooms is a great summertime activity for food lovers. Chanterelles are susceptible to weather conditions and can sometimes be quite wet. If so, spread them out in a single layer on a baking sheet and leave them on a counter overnight. As fun and exciting as it is to pick wild mushrooms, always do so with an experienced forager or with a mushroom guidebook.

Strudel

2 lb (900 g) fresh, cleaned chanterelle mushrooms
3 shallots, minced
1 clove garlic, minced
1 tsp (5 mL) salt
1 tsp (5 mL) freshly ground black pepper
¼ cup (60 mL) butter
¼ cup (60 mL) dry sherry
2 tbsp (30 mL) chopped fresh sage
2 tbsp (30 mL) chopped fresh parsley
½ cup (125 mL) breadcrumbs
1 package frozen puff pastry dough, thawed
1 egg
2 tbsp (30 mL) milk
1 tbsp (15 mL) fleur de sel or kosher salt
½ cup (125 mL) Greek yogurt

Spinach sauce

1 shallot, minced
¼ tsp (1 mL) grated lemon zest
1 tbsp (15 mL) butter
1 (8 oz/225 g) bag cleaned spinach
6 leaves fresh basil
½ cup (125 mL) white wine
½ cup (125 mL) heavy cream (35% m.f.)
1 tsp (5 mL) lemon juice
⅛ tsp (0.5 mL) freshly grated nutmeg
salt and pepper, to taste

For the strudel: Slice any large chanterelle mushrooms in two or three pieces. Smaller mushrooms can be left whole. Sauté mushrooms, shallots, garlic, salt and pepper in butter until mushrooms release their water. Lower the heat and cook for a further 10 minutes until water evaporates and the pan is dry. Deglaze the pan with sherry. Add fresh herbs and breadcrumbs and stir into mushrooms. Remove from heat and allow to cool completely in the refrigerator.

Roll out puff pastry dough into a rectangle, 8 x 11 in (20 x 27 cm). Place cooled filling in the centre along the long axis. Make an eggwash with egg and milk and brush along the inside seam of the dough. This will help seal the dough as it bakes. Roll the strudel over so the seam is underneath. Brush the top with eggwash, sprinkle with fleur de sel or kosher salt and make 4 angled slits in the top with a knife. This will ventilate the strudel as it bakes.

Bake in a 400°F (200°C) oven for 20 minutes, or until dough is a deep brown colour and feels crisp to the touch. Allow to rest for 10 minutes before serving.

For the spinach sauce: Sweat shallot and lemon zest in butter. Increase heat under the pan and add spinach and basil. Sauté until just wilted and add wine. Reduce by half. Add cream, lemon juice and nutmeg and bring just to the boil. Purée in a blender and adjust seasoning with a little salt and pepper if desired. Serve immediately. If you are making the sauce in advance and wish to use it later, cool the purée over an ice bath as quickly as possible to preserve the lovely green colour. Also, depending on the time of year and variety of spinach, the thickness of the sauce may vary. You can always add a few drops of chicken stock or even water if it appears too thick.

Slice strudel into 6 to 8 pieces, depending on the desired portion size. Serve with warm spinach sauce and a tablespoon of thick Greek yogurt.

Serves 6 to 8

Seared Quebec Foie Gras on a Cheddar Chive Biscuit with Balsamic Glazed Plums

The ultimate in luxury and decadence, seared foie gras from Quebec needs little special attention, only a hot pan and some good salt. The idea here was to put a "down home" biscuit twist on the traditional brioche accompaniment to the liver. The plums are both tart and sweet and stand up well to the richness of the duck liver. Locally-grown plums from farmers' markets are normally superior to those sold in large stores.

6 Cheddar Chive Biscuits (see modified buttermilk biscuit recipe
   in "Basics" chapter)
1 ½ cups (375 mL) halved plums
2 tbsp (30 mL) unsalted butter
¼ cup (60 mL) Maple Balsamic Syrup (recipe in "Basics" chapter)
1 lb (450 g) grade A foie gras
1 tbsp (15 mL) fleur de sel

Heat biscuits in a 300°F (150°C) oven before serving.

In a sauté pan, cook plums in butter for 3 minutes and then add Maple Balsamic Syrup. Cook for 5 minutes on low heat and then store in a sealed container. Plums can be served warm or cold.

Heat a nonstick frying pan to high. Slice the lobe of foie gras into 6 pieces, approximately 2 ½ to 3 oz (70 to 85 g) each. Score the top of each slice with the tip of a paring knife, about ¹⁄₁₆-in (1-mm) deep, in a cross pattern. Sear liver on each side for about 30 seconds. The pan will smoke a little but that's normal. Carefully remove from the pan and place a slice of foie gras on the bottom half of a warm biscuit. Sprinkle with fleur de sel and garnish with several plum halves.

Serves 6

Tuna Pizza "Nicoise" with Lemon Caper Aioli

Pizzas in Italy are baked in an intensely hot wood-fired oven and often garnished with fresh ingredients just before serving. Some examples of these ingredients include fresh arugula, proscuitto, basil, cured pork fat (known as lardo) and even carpaccio of beef. This is a fun and casual way to enjoy properly cooked tuna on a pizza but the tuna must be absolutely fresh. Serving it in the style of the famous Salade Nicoise crosses two wonderful Italian and French peasant dishes.

Pizza
14 oz (400 g) pizza dough (see recipe in Basics)
1 cup (250 mL) crushed tomatoes or canned organic pizza sauce
½ cup (125 mL) sliced red onions
1 ripe tomato, thinly sliced
½ cup (125 mL) pitted black kalamata olives
1 green zucchini, sliced

Aioli
2 cloves garlic, peeled, germ removed
juice and zest of 1 lemon
1 tbsp (15 mL) capers
2 egg yolks
½ tsp (3 mL) salt
½ tsp (3 mL) hot sauce
1 cup (250 mL) pomace or light olive oil

Tuna
3 tbsp (45 mL) extra-virgin olive oil
1 tbsp (15 mL) dried oregano
1 tbsp (15 mL) chopped parsley
1 tsp (5 mL) freshly ground black pepper
1 x 12 oz (300 g) fresh tuna loin

Preheat oven to 500°F (260°C).

For the pizza: Roll out pizza dough into two 12-inch (30-cm) diameter rounds. Divide all ingredients equally between both pizzas and bake on a pizza stone for 5 to 7 minutes or until crust is crisp and browned on the underside.

For the lemon caper aioli: Pulse garlic, lemon juice, zest, capers, egg yolks, salt and hot sauce in a food processor. Once in a paste, slowly add olive oil in a steady stream. If aioli "breaks" (i.e. the oil and liquids separate and look "curdled") stop machine, add a couple of drops of water and mix with a hand whisk to re-emulsify. Chill aioli in the refrigerator.

For the tuna: In a mixing bowl, combine olive oil, herbs and pepper and mix well. Gently roll tuna in the seasoned oil and preheat a nonstick pan over medium-high heat. Sear the tuna on all sides until it is golden in colour. Each side will take about 45 seconds to 1 minute. Set aside on a resting rack.

To serve the pizza, slice tuna thinly and place on top of cooked crust. Garnish with dollops of lemon caper aioli.

Serves 6 to 8

Fruits de Mer Salad with Sauce Marie Rose

Sauce Marie Rose is the European equivalent of North America's cocktail sauce. For this salad appetizer I find that its smoothness enhances the different textures and flavours of the seafood more than the sharp horseradish heat of a traditional seafood sauce. You can serve this dish as a salad on some Boston lettuce leaves, in a martini glass or on a large platter garnished with watercress or fresh basil leaves. Use only the very freshest seafood from your local fishmonger.

Salad

6 cups (1.5 L) water
3 cups (750 mL) dry white wine
1 medium onion, coarsely chopped
1 carrot, coarsely chopped
1 stalk celery, coarsely chopped
1 lemon, halved
3 bay leaves
3 sprigs fresh thyme
1 x 2 lb (900 g) lobster
12 sea scallops (10/20 count)
18 tiger prawns (20/30 count)
12 choice oysters, shucked
1 lb (450 g) calamari sliced into ¼-in (6-mm) rings
1 cup (250 mL) Sauce Marie Rose (recipe follows)
¼ cup (60 mL) sliced chives

Sauce marie rose

1 cup (250 mL) mayonnaise
½ cup (125 mL) tomato ketchup
1 tsp (5 mL) lemon juice
¼ tsp (1 mL) salt
1 tbsp (15 mL) Worcestershire sauce
1 tsp (5 mL) Tabasco or your favourite hot sauce
1 tbsp (15 mL) brandy or dry sherry

For the salad: In a stockpot, place water, wine, onion, carrot, celery, lemon, bay leaves and thyme and bring to a boil. As soon as the liquid boils drop in the live lobster and cook, covered, for 12 minutes. Remove lobster and refrigerate until cool. Lower the temperature of the cooking liquid to a simmer and poach each type of seafood until just cooked but not rubbery. Depending on the size of the ingredients, each should take between 1 and 3 minutes. The calamari will take the shortest time and the scallops will take the longest. Remove seafood from cooking liquid and spread it out on a baking sheet. Refrigerate right away to prevent residual cooking as much as possible.

When ready to serve, remove seafood from refrigerator and place in a bowl with Sauce Marie Rose. Clean lobster and cut tail meat and claws into 1-inch (2.5-cm) pieces. Toss all ingredients together and garnish with sliced chives.

Serves 6

For the sauce: Combine all ingredients in a bowl and whisk until smooth.

Yields 1 ½ cups (375 mL)

Brown Sugar–braised Bacon with Navy Bean, Kale, Celery and Horseradish Ragout

In 2004 I drove across Canada seeking new cooking experiences by working with some of the most creative chefs in the country. It was at Canoe in Toronto that I first tried Chef Antony Walsh's "Canoe Bacon." Since that first heavenly taste of bacon cooked slowly and served creamy and moist I have experimented with different cures and methods of cooking before getting it right.

Braised bacon

1 ½ cups (375 mL) brown sugar
½ cup (125 mL) rock salt
1 tbsp (15 mL) ground cinnamon
1 tbsp (15 mL) whole cloves
1 pod star anise
1 tbsp (15 mL) cracked peppercorns
½ full pork belly, skin removed (approximately 2 ½ lb or 1 kg)
2 cups (500 mL) Demi Glace (see recipe in "Basics" chapter)
1 cup (250 mL) low-sodium beef broth
1 cup (250 mL) dry sherry
1 small onion, coarsely chopped
1 stalk celery, coarsely chopped
3 bay leaves
1 cinnamon stick
2 cloves garlic, whole
½ cup (125 mL) molasses

Ragout

1 cup (250 mL) diced celery root (½-in/1-cm cubes)
3 tbsp olive oil
½ stalk celery, minced
1 small onion, minced
1 clove garlic
1 tsp (5 mL) salt
1 tsp (5 mL) pepper
¼ cup (60 mL) white wine
1 can white navy beans, rinsed
2 cups (500 mL) cleaned and chopped kale leaves
1 cup (250 mL) bacon braising liquid (reserved from braising recipe)
¼ cup (60 mL) fresh celery leaves
2 tbsp (30 mL) freshly grated fresh horseradish (NOTE: Fresh horseradish can be found in top grocery stores near the root vegetables and is grated just like parmesan cheese or fresh ginger)

For the braised bacon: In a bowl, combine brown sugar, rock salt, cinnamon, cloves, star anise and cracked peppercorns and mix well. Place one-half of the spice rub in the bottom of a casserole dish and set pork belly on top. Cover belly with the remaining spice mix and refrigerate, covered, for 48 hours.

Remove pork belly from the casserole and brush off cloves and peppercorns. Place in a clean roasting pan or appropriately sized casserole dish.

In a saucepan, bring demi glace, beef broth, sherry, onion, celery, bay leaves, cinnamon stick, garlic and molasses to a boil. (Store-bought powdered demi glace mixed with water will make a fine substitute for homemade.) As soon as the liquid boils remove from heat and pour over pork belly. Make sure belly is completely submerged in liquid before it goes into the oven. Use a resting rack as a weight if need be.

Cook pork belly overnight in a 175°F (80°C) oven for a minimum of 12 hours. When fork-tender remove from oven and allow to cool in the liquid. When the liquid is cold and congealed remove the belly and wipe off any excess braising liquid. Reserve liquid. Place belly on a roasting rack with the fat cap facing upwards. Broil the belly until the fat cap is well browned. Lower the broil heat after a couple of minutes to render out more fat, making the bacon less greasy. Refrigerate belly once more until firm and slice into 2-oz (60-g) portions, about 1 ½ x 1 ½ in (4 x 4 cm).

The braising liquid can be heated and strained and used as an accompanying sauce to the pork.

For the ragout: In a preheated saucepan, pan roast celery root in olive oil over medium high heat until lightly brown. Add celery, onion, garlic, salt and pepper and cook over medium heat for 5 minutes. Deglaze the pan with white wine and cook until dry. Add navy beans, kale and reserved braising liquid and simmer for 30 minutes on low heat.

To serve ragout and bacon together simply reheat bacon in the microwave until warmed through. Place on top of a spoonful of ragout and drizzle a little more braising liquid over the top. Garnish with celery leaves and freshly grated horseradish.

Serves 8, with some leftover braised bacon

Crispy Duck Confit with Head Lettuce and Cider Vinaigrette

To confit means to cook slowly, immersed in fat usually from the same source as the item being prepared, both for flavour and preservation. It is one of the oldest means of preserving meat. The duck confit in the following dish can be used in numerous ways, but this simple preparation calls for the duck legs to be re-crisped in a pan and served warm on a simple salad of garden greens. Fantastic duck comes from Quebec but many small farms raise free-range birds as well. Ask around and you may get lucky.

Confit

6 tbsp (90 mL) coarse or kosher salt
4 bay leaves, finely crushed
1 tsp (5 mL) powdered clove
1 tsp (5 mL) crushed star anise
1 tsp (5 mL) cracked black peppercorns
6 duck legs
3 lb (1.35 kg) duck fat
2 sprigs fresh sage
2 sprigs fresh thyme
1 sprig fresh rosemary

Cider vinaigrette

2 cups (500 mL) apple cider
¼ cup (60 mL) honey
1 shallot, minced
2 sprigs fresh tarragon
¼ cup (60 mL) cider vinegar
1 tsp (5 mL) dry mustard
1 apple, peeled and minced
2 tbsp (30 mL) chopped fresh tarragon
2 tbsp (30 mL) chopped chives
⅛ tsp (0.5 mL) salt
⅛ tsp (0.5 mL) pepper
1 ½ cups (375 mL) light olive oil or cold-pressed canola oil
1 large head of your favourite lettuce

For the confit: Mix salt and dry spices together and rub mixture into duck legs. Refrigerate legs on a resting rack overnight to cure. Brush off spices and pat legs dry with paper towels. In a saucepan, melt duck fat until just warm. Place duck legs snugly in the bottom of a lasagna or casserole dish. Place sage, thyme and rosemary in the fat and pour over the legs. Cook gently over very low heat for about 2 hours or until meat is fork tender. This can also be done in an oven at 300°F.

To store the confit simply allow the fat to congeal around the legs in the refrigerator. You can keep them for up to 6 weeks this way.

For the cider vinaigrette: Bring apple cider, honey, shallot and tarragon sprigs to a boil in a saucepan and reduce by one-half. Allow to fully cool. Add reduced cider to a mixing bowl along with cider vinegar, mustard, minced apple, chopped herbs, salt, and pepper. Slowly whisk in the oil.

To assemble salad, clean lettuce. I like to use whole leaves as this salad is really a "knife and fork" dish, being served with a whole leg of duck. Using a nonstick frying pan, reheat chilled duck legs over medium heat until skin goes crisp. Toss greens in vinaigrette, using about 1 ½ fluid ounces (30 mL) per serving. To serve, place one duck leg on greens and garnish with dried or fresh apple slices.

Serves 6

Shrimp Toast with Roasted Organic Garlic

At Chives, we have recently embraced a sustainable trap-caught shrimp fishery here in Nova Scotia and this seemed to be the perfect dish to showcase the luxurious ingredient. The shrimp comes whole, as served in Europe, which is a bit of a new concept for Canadians. However, cleaning them is easy and the taste is incredible. I have made a shrimp bisque with the shells and used that soup base as a base for my shrimp toast in this recipe.

Shrimp toast

6 slices sourdough or French baguette
3 tbsp (45 mL) extra-virgin olive oil
1 head garlic
2 lb (900 g) fresh trap-caught shrimp, cleaned and shells reserved
2 shallots, minced
3 tbsp (45 mL) butter
¼ cup (60 mL) sherry
1 cup (250 mL) Shrimp Bisque (recipe follows)
¼ cup (60 mL) heavy cream (35% m.f.)
¼ cup (60 mL) grated Parmesan cheese
⅛ cup (30 mL) roughly chopped Italian parsley

Shrimp bisque *

shrimp shells, reserved from recipe above
1 medium onion, coarsely chopped
1 stalk celery, coarsely chopped
1 clove garlic
1 medium carrot, coarsely chopped
1 tsp (5 mL) salt
1 tsp (5 mL) pepper
2 tbsp (30 mL) olive oil
½ cup (125 mL) dry sherry
1 cup (250 mL) diced fresh tomato
3 cups (750 mL) fish or chicken broth
2 stalks fresh thyme
2 bay leaves

Brush bread with olive oil and grill on barbecue until golden. A few charred bits are great — they add a smoky flavour to the dish.

For the shrimp toast: Bake whole head of garlic in a 350°F (180°C) oven for 35 minutes. When cooled, cut off ¼ inch (0.5 cm) from the plant or bulbous end of the head and squeeze out the cloves. Mash with a fork to create a purée.

In a large pan, sauté shrimp, shallots and garlic purée in butter for 3 minutes. Remove shrimp from the pan and reserve for a few minutes on a side dish. Place the pan back on the heat and deglaze with sherry, reducing the original volume by two-thirds. Add bisque and cream and bring to the boil. When sauce looks smooth and creamy return shrimp to pan and toss with Parmesan and Italian parsley. Divide shrimp evenly over hot grilled bread and serve immediately.

Serves 6

For the shrimp bisque: In a saucepan, sauté shrimp shells, onion, celery, garlic, carrot, salt, and pepper in olive oil. Cook until vegetables are translucent and shells are pink. Deglaze the pan with sherry and cook until pan is dry. Add diced tomato, broth and fresh herbs and simmer for 1 hour. Purée soup in a blender, including shells, and strain through a chinois into a clean bowl. Refrigerate until needed.

* With fresh shrimp and a touch of cream, this is a great soup on a cold autumn day, accompanied with crusty French bread.

Yields 5 cups (1.25 L)

Smoked Salmon Tartar with Pickled Cucumber, Sour Cream and Chives

This dish can be presented, as I describe it here, simply on a piece of pumpernickel as a lunch or brunch item. When I serve it as an hors d'oeuvre I use a small cookie cutter about 1 ½ inches (4 cm) in diameter to make a base of toasted pumpernickel bread, then stack each element on top, alternating layers of salmon, cucumber and crème fraiche. The result is a stunning and elegant way to start a dinner party. No matter how it is served — simple or formal — it is just as flavourful. Go for locally produced artisan-smoked salmon if possible.

½ English cucumber, cut in half lengthwise
½ tsp (3 mL) salt
2 tbsp (15 mL) rice wine vinegar
2 tbsp (15 mL) chopped fresh dill
8 oz (225 g) quality artisan-smoked salmon
3 tbsp chopped Pickled Red Onions (see recipe in "Pickles and
   Preserves" chapter)
juice of ½ lemon
1 tbsp (15 mL) chopped capers
4 slices toasted rye or pumpernickel bread
2 tbsp (30 mL) butter
½ cup (125 mL) sour cream
4 tbsp (60 mL) chopped chives

Remove seeds from cucumber, slice thinly and place in a small strainer. Each slice should resemble a "half moon." Mix in salt and rest strainer over a bowl for 2 hours. The salt will cause the cucumber to release its water into the bowl. Pat cucumber slices dry with a paper towel and place in a clean bowl with rice wine vinegar and chopped dill. Adjust seasoning if required.

Finely chop smoked salmon and place in a mixing bowl with onions, lemon juice and chopped capers. Using a 4-inch (10-cm) diameter cookie cutter make 4 rounds of rye or pumpernickel and butter lightly on one side. Spread salmon mixture evenly over toast using a small metal spatula or knife. Pile pickled cucumbers in the centre of the toast, garnish with a spoonful of sour cream and sprinkle with chopped chives.

Serves 4

Mushroom and White Cheddar Tartlet with Baby Lettuce and Poached-garlic Vinaigrette

All the ingredients in this recipe should be available year-round in any part of Canada. In my neck of the woods I choose local log-raised mushrooms and cloth-aged cheddar from Prince Edward Island. This dish is really a type of puff pastry pizza and can be served as an appetizer or a main course. You can even cut very small "crusts" of dough about 2 inches (5 cm) in diameter and use them as hors d'oeuvres.

Tartlet

2 cups (500 mL) sliced portobello mushrooms
2 cups (500 mL) sliced button mushrooms
2 cups (500 mL) sliced shiitake mushrooms
2 cups (500 mL) halved oyster mushrooms
3 shallots, minced
2 cloves garlic, minced
¼ cup (60 mL) extra-virgin olive oil
2 tsp (10 mL) salt
1 tsp (5 mL) pepper
½ cup (125 mL) port wine
½ cup (125 mL) Sauce Bianco (recipe follows)
1 frozen puff pastry crust
2 cups (500 mL) grated aged white cheddar
2 cups (500 mL) baby greens or mesclun mix
¼ cup (60 mL) Poached Garlic Vinaigrette (recipe follows)

Sauce bianco

1 cup (250 mL) milk
½ tsp (3 mL) salt
1 tsp (5 mL) pepper
2 cloves garlic, minced
1 tbsp (15 mL) white wine
1 tbsp (15 mL) minced shallot
1 tsp (5 mL) dried oregano
2 tbsp (30 mL) Parmesan cheese
1 tbsp (15 mL) cornstarch
1 tbsp (15 mL) water

Poached-garlic vinaigrette

1 ½ cups (375 mL) extra-virgin olive oil
1 cup (250 mL) garlic cloves
½ cup (125 mL) white balsamic vinegar
¼ cup (60 mL) chopped chives
¼ cup (60 mL) minced red pepper
1 tsp (5 mL) salt
1 tsp (5 mL) pepper

For the tartlet: In a large saucepan, cook mushrooms, shallots and garlic in oil with salt and pepper. When mushrooms release their liquid they will reduce in volume. Deglaze the pan with port wine and continue cooking over medium/low heat until all the liquid evaporates. Allow mushrooms to cool completely before assembling the tart.

Spread Sauce Bianco on the puff dough and place mushrooms on top. Cover in cheddar cheese and bake at 425°F (215°C) for 12 minutes, or until bottom of crust is golden brown. Serve with a small salad of baby greens tossed in Poached-garlic Vinaigrette.

Serves 4 to 6

For the Sauce Bianco: Combine all ingredients except cornstarch and water in a small saucepan and bring to a simmer. Cook for 15 minutes over low heat. Make a slurry of cornstarch and water and add to the sauce to thicken. Never allow sauce to boil, or the milk will curdle. Refrigerate until needed.

Yields 1 ¼ cups (310 mL)

For the vinaigrette: In a saucepan, heat olive oil and poach whole garlic cloves in oil for 1 hour on medium/low heat. Remove cloves from oil and roughly chop with a knife. Add garlic back to oil along with remaining ingredients. Whisk well and refrigerate for 24 hours before using to allow flavours to meld. Vinaigrette can be stored for up to 3 weeks in a sealed container.

Yields 2 ½ cups (625 mL)

Fried Feta Cheese with Grilled Winter Vegetable Salsa

The difference between good and bad feta, in my opinion, is in balance. The cheese needs to be firm yet still crumbly, salty but not too much and silky smooth on the palate. I have found a feta cheese just like that in the Annapolis Valley and good quality locally made fetas are available at a growing number of specialty stores. Grilled vegetable salsa is a fun reason to fire up the barbecue during the cold winter months.

Fried feta

½ cup (125 mL) canola oil or light olive oil
2 eggs
3 tbsp (45 mL) milk
6 x 3-oz (90-g) pieces feta cheese (cut into triangles or rectangles)
¼ cup (60 mL) flour
1 cup (250 mL) panko (Japanese) breadcrumbs

Salsa

2 medium-sized carrots
1 parsnip
1 green zucchini
1 red onion
½ anise bulb
8 tbsp (120 mL) extra-virgin olive oil
1 tsp (5 mL) salt
1 tsp (5 mL) pepper
½ red pepper
½ yellow pepper
2 cloves garlic, minced
2 tbsp (30 mL) chopped fresh oregano
2 tbsp (30 mL) chopped parsley
4 tbsp white balsamic or aged sherry vinegar

For the fried feta: Preheat canola oil in a steep-sided saucepan and, using a fry thermometer, hold the temperature of the oil at 350°F (180°C). In a bowl, mix eggs and milk together. Dredge each piece of cheese in flour, then in mixture of egg and milk and finally in breadcrumbs. Fry each piece carefully in oil until crisp and golden, about 3 minutes.

For the salsa: Preheat barbecue grill on high. Thinly slice carrots, parsnip, and zucchini into ribbons and slice onion and anise thinly into disks. Toss vegetables in a mixing bowl with 4 tablespoons of olive oil, salt and pepper. Grill each slice until grill-marked and lightly charred but not too dark. Char peppers skin side towards the heat until the skin blisters and turns black. Place in a bowl covered with cling film. Rest for 20 minutes until cool to the touch. The pepper can be easily peeled at this point leaving only the sweet flesh of the pepper for the salsa. When all the vegetables are grilled, allow to cool and then dice as finely as possible — a good size is about ⅛-in (3-mm) cubes. Toss diced vegetables in remaining olive oil, minced garlic, herbs and vinegar. Adjust seasoning as desired and set aside.

Serve immediately with a large spoonful of vegetable salsa over the top of each piece of cheese.

Serves 6

Hot-Smoked Sea Trout on Rosti Potato with Beetroot Salad

Sea trout is available year-round because it is a farmed product. During the summer, serving this fish with beautiful baby beets — both golden and deep purple in colour — is the way to go. Using beets from the cold cellar in winter is just as nice, especially when slow-roasted in the oven.

Fish
4 x 7-oz (200-g) trout fillets, skin on, bones removed
1 cup (250 mL) maple wood chips
4 tsp (20 mL) butter
1 tbsp (15 mL) fleur de sel

Potatoes
4 medium-sized Yukon Gold potatoes
3 tbsp (45 mL) salt
1 cup (250 mL) butter
2 tsp (10 mL) salt (second amount)
2 tsp (10 mL) pepper

Beet salad
1 ½ cups (375 mL) diced golden beets
1 ½ cups (375 mL) diced red beets
4 tbsp (60 mL) extra-virgin olive oil
1 small shallot, minced
juice and zest of ½ lemon
1 tbsp (15 mL) chopped dill
½ tsp (3 mL) salt

For the fish: On the barbecue, or using a stovetop roasting pan, place trout fillets on a resting rack directly over wood chips. Smoke over high heat for 5 to 6 minutes. Once wood chips have blackened and released most of their smoke, remove trout and place each piece skin side up directly on 1 teaspoon of butter. Roast fillet in a 400°F (200°C) oven for 4 minutes or until it is just cooked in the middle. Before serving, peel away the skin and season trout with a little fleur de sel.

For the rosti potatoes: Boil potatoes with their skins on in water with 3 tablespoons of salt. The potatoes should be al dente, or about 75 percent cooked. Allow to cool fully, then peel and grate on the large side of a hand grater. In a small saucepan, heat butter until it just melts. Set aside for 15 minutes to allow the water and milk solids to separate.

Using a spoon skim off the floating milk solids, then carefully ladle the clear butter fat off the separated water.

Heat 4 tablespoons of clarified butter in a nonstick pan. Using a circular ring mould or cookie cutter 4 in (10 cm) in diameter, make small potato pancakes with grated potato, packing it well with your fingers. Each rosti should be about ⅜-in (1-cm) thick. Season with a little salt and pepper and pan fry until golden. It may be necessary to add a little more butter after the rosti are flipped, as they will absorb butter while they cook.

For the beet salad: Toss beets in 3 tablespoons (45 mL) of olive oil and roast in a 350°F (180°C) oven for 15 minutes. In a small bowl, mix shallots, lemon juice and zest, dill, salt and remaining olive oil. Add beets and allow to marinate for 1 hour before serving.

To serve the dish, place a rosti in the center of a warmed luncheon plate. Make a small pile of beet salad and top with trout. Garnish with fresh herbs or baby greens like radish sprouts, mustard, or arugula.

Serves 4

Pasta, Risotto & Side Dishes

I am utterly fascinated by the history and traditions behind handmade pasta, ravioli and gnocchi. I equally enjoy the regional histories of dishes like "hodge podge" and the numerous ways root vegetables and potatoes are prepared in the Maritimes.

The dishes in this chapter are the humble man's dinners of Northern Italy, Nova Scotia's Pictou County and the Okanagan Valley. These are the dishes I enjoy cooking more than any others.

Risotto, the creamy rice dish originating from the Po River Valley in Piedmont, Italy, is my absolute favourite to prepare. The richness and flavour of the rice is compelling enough on its own, but the grains also become a vehicle for other flavours. I find risotto-making a cathartic and relaxing experience. It forces me to slow down and pay close attention to the dish I am creating. It reminds me why I became a chef.

The key point to remember when making any of these dishes is to pick a theme and stick with it. If there are too many flavours, they will compete for your attention and ruin the experience. Only one or two key ingredients are required when you have taken the time to make things from scratch.

The other side dishes highlighted here will make great additions to your home pantry collection of recipes. Potatoes, squash and root vegetables are common in Canadian kitchens and should be celebrated, not treated as boring "go to" starches to be served alongside a plate of dry roast pork. They have sustained civilizations for centuries and — more importantly — they are delicious.

Caramelized Sea Scallops with Westphalian Ham, Swiss Chard, Lovage and Lemon Risotto

Once you taste this dish you will recognize it immediately. The familiar flavours of scallops and smoky bacon are recreated here by using Westphalian ham. If you can't get Westphalian ham, use a double-smoked bacon made locally. The smoky flavour is key here so I would avoid using regular ham. Swiss chard is a great ingredient to grow in a small garden. Bright and resilient in the cold, it continues to yield even after the first cutting. Swiss chard is often baked with bacon in Europe as a side dish.

5 cups (1.25 L) low-sodium chicken broth (freshly made is preferable)
1 medium onion, minced
2 cloves garlic
1 stalk celery, minced
1 tsp (5 mL) salt
1 tsp (5 mL) pepper
¼ cup (60 mL) butter
⅛ cup (30 mL) extra-virgin olive oil
¾ cup (180 mL) minced Westphalian ham
1 10/30 cups (375 mL) Italian Arborio or Caranoli rice
1 cup (250 mL) dry white wine or vermouth
2 cups (500 mL) packed and chopped yellow or white-stemmed Swiss chard
juice and zest of 1 lemon
1 cup (250 mL) grated Parmesan cheese
¼ cup (60 mL) cold butter
2 lb (1 kg) sea scallops (10-20 count)
¼ cup (60 mL) olive oil or vegetable oil
1 tbsp (15 mL) fleur de sel
freshly ground black pepper
2 tbsp (30 mL) chopped chives

In a stockpot, heat chicken stock to a simmer.

In a separate heavy-bottomed rondeau or stockpot, sauté onion, garlic, celery, salt and pepper in the butter and extra-virgin olive oil for 10 minutes. Keep the heat at medium-high and stir often. If garlic begins to brown too quickly, lower the heat and add a few drops of water. Add ham and rice next, stirring constantly in order to coat rice grains with oil. After a few minutes the rice will begin to look translucent. At this point add wine.

The real process of risotto-making begins here. The liquid must be added slowly in stages and cooked into the grains completely before adding more, or the rice will slowly begin to release its starch and thicken the surrounding stock, which increases the likelihood of sticking. You must stay with the risotto the entire time you are preparing the dish.

Cook wine out completely, until the pot is dry. Begin adding heated stock in about 1-cup (250-mL) increments. The risotto will take about 15 to 18 minutes to become al dente — the rice is cooked but still gives some resistance to the tooth when bitten.

Add Swiss chard when the liquid is about 75 percent absorbed. Complete the cooking and remove from the heat. Add lemon juice and zest, cheese and butter while the risotto is resting.

Preheat a nonstick sauté pan to high. Dry scallops on a paper towel, and remove the tough adductor muscle on the side before cooking. Add oil to the pan and sear each scallop on the flat side for 2 minutes. Turn each scallop once and immediately remove from the heat. The residual heat in the pan will complete the cooking in about 3 minutes. Sprinkle each scallop with a little fleur de sel and a grind of black pepper. As an alternative, the scallops can be skewered and grilled on a barbecue. The cooking times remain much the same but the scallops should be brushed with a little olive oil before grilling.

To serve, spoon the risotto onto a plate or into a large soup bowl. Place scallops on top (about 6 per person) and garnish with chopped chives.

Serves 6

Pancetta, Asparagus and Pattypan Squash with Traditional Alfredo Sauce

The incredible thing about this recipe is how quickly it comes together. From start to finish you can make this dish in about 10 minutes, while the pasta is cooking in the pot. Traditional Alfredo sauce is nothing more than egg yolks, cream and Parmesan cheese. The technique is key. The sauce thickens as the egg yolk cooks in the heat of the pasta alone. Local asparagus and squash are two items that always seem to be carried in larger grocery chain stores, much to my delight.

Alfredo sauce
3 egg yolks
1 cup (250 mL) heavy cream (35% m.f.)
1 cup (125 mL) grated Parmesan cheese
½ tsp (1 mL) salt
½ tsp (1 mL) freshly ground black pepper

Pasta
3 cups (750 mL) dry penne rigate pasta
1 shallot, minced
4 cloves garlic, minced
2 cups (500 mL) halved pattypan squash
8 slices pancetta (Italian bacon), chopped
3 tbsp (45 mL) butter
2 tbsp (30 mL) extra-virgin olive oil
1 lb (450 g) asparagus, sliced into 2-in (5-cm) pieces
4 stalks fresh thyme, leaves removed, stalks discarded
1 tsp (5 mL) freshly ground black pepper
Italian parsley, for garnish

For the Alfredo sauce: Combine all ingredients in a small bowl and whisk until smooth. Set aside.

For the pasta: Bring a pot of salted water to the boil and cook penne following the instructions on the package, taking care not to overcook it. Most dry pasta is ready in 6 or 7 minutes if the water is at a full boil. In a large sauté pan, cook shallots, garlic, squash and pancetta in butter and oil for 3 minutes over medium-high heat. Add asparagus and fresh thyme and cook for an additional 3 minutes. Season with black pepper. Avoid adding salt to the dish until this point, as the saltiness of pancetta varies. Remove the pan from the heat and allow to rest for 2 minutes.

Add cooked penne and toss well. Add Alfredo sauce and stir with a wooden spoon. The heat of the pasta will cause the egg yolks to "grab" the sauce and make it rich and creamy.

Serve immediately, garnished with a sprinkle of extra cheese, olive oil or some chopped Italian parsley.

Serves 4

Lamb, Parmesan and Mint Croquettes

The great beauty of this dish is that it uses leftover risotto and lamb. When a risotto has been fully cooked and cooled it is impossible to reheat it by adding stock. The grains just turn to mush and the dish loses its appeal. A croquette, however, disturbs each grain much less during reheating. I use leftover braised lamb shanks or pot roast here for the meat. These croquettes make a delicious treat when served with a simple tossed green salad or tomato sauce.

3 cups (750 mL) cold basic risotto (see recipe in "Basics")
1 ½ cups (325 mL) picked cold braised lamb shank or shoulder,
   picked into small pieces
1 cup (250 mL) grated Parmesan cheese
4 tbsp (60 mL) chopped mint
3 eggs
3 tbsp (45 mL) water
¼ tsp (1 mL) salt
¼ tsp (1 mL) pepper
1 cup (250 mL) flour
2 cups (500 mL) panko or Italian breadcrumbs
6 cups (1.5 L) vegetable oilIn a mixing bowl, combine cold risotto, lamb, cheese and mint and gently mix together. Form into croquettes 2 in (5 cm) in diameter.

In a small bowl, beat eggs, water, salt and pepper until combined. Dredge each croquette in flour, then eggwash and finally breadcrumbs. Heat vegetable oil in a steep-sided pot to 350°F (180°C). Measure the temperature with a fry thermometer to ensure accuracy. Fry croquettes until golden brown, approximately 3 minutes per croquette.

Serve immediately while crisp and hot.

Serves 6

Mushroom and Olive Oil Confit, Goat's Cheese and Thyme Risotto

For this dish I suggest using the base recipe for risotto in *Basics* modified with the goat's cheese and thyme. The mushroom confit is the element that should be showcased here by sprinkling the mushrooms over the top of the risotto. Slow-cooking in scented olive oil keeps the moisture inside the mushrooms and prevents them from going rubbery.

2 lb (900 g) mixed mushrooms such as button, cremini,
  portobello, chanterelle, shiitake and oyster, cleaned and
  stems removed
2 shallots, cut in half
4 cloves garlic, cut in half
4 bay leaves
4 sprigs fresh thyme
2 sprigs fresh rosemary
8 cups (2 L) extra-virgin olive oil

Combine all ingredients in a deep baking dish, covering mushrooms and vegetables with olive oil. It is essential that the oil covers all the mushrooms. Cover with tin foil and place in a 200°F (100°C) oven for 3 hours.

For the risotto, replace the Parmesan cheese in the base recipe (see recipe in "Basics") with 1 cup (250 mL) creamy goat's cheese and 4 tbsp (60 mL) fresh thyme leaves.

Serve warm mushrooms seasoned with a little salt and freshly ground black pepper over the risotto.

Serves 6 to 8

Garden Vegetable Fusilli with Smoked Tomato Sauce and Olives

Smoking tomatoes may seem to be a nuisance at first, but it is a great way to complement the vegetables without adding extra fat. I do not use cheese here, because I find that so many *pasta primavera* dishes are boring, but go right ahead if you like. This recipe features readily available vegetables that are grown locally right across Canada. Carnivores can add some sausage, grilled chicken or even lamb to this dish and make a really hearty meal out of it.

Vegetable fusilli

1 small red onion, sliced
3 cloves garlic, minced
1 red pepper, julienned
1 yellow pepper, julienned
1 cup (250 mL) sugar snap peas
1 small yellow zucchini, sliced ½ in (12 mm) thick
½ lb (220 g) asparagus, chopped into 2-in (5-cm) pieces
1 cup (250 mL) cherry tomatoes
¼ cup (60 mL) extra-virgin olive oil
1 tsp (5 mL) salt
1 tsp (5 mL) hot sauce
4 cups (1 L) Smoked Tomato Sauce (recipe follows)
4 cups (1 L) cooked fusilli pasta
2 cups (500 mL) packed spinach
½ cup (125 mL) grated Parmesan for garnish

Smoked tomato sauce

6 large ripe red field tomatoes (about 2 lb/1 kg total weight)
½ cup maple wood chips
1 cup (250 mL) minced onion
4 cloves garlic, minced
½ cup (125 mL) minced celery
1 tsp (5 mL) dried basil
1 tsp (5 mL) dried oregano
½ tsp (3 mL) chili flakes
½ tsp (3 mL) salt
1 tsp (5 mL) freshly ground black pepper
½ cup (125 mL) extra-virgin olive oil
1 cup (250 mL) red wine
½ cup (125 mL) sun-dried tomatoes
1 tbsp (15 mL) brown sugar
2 cups (500 mL) organic tomato juice

For the vegetable fusilli: Sauté all vegetables (except spinach) in olive oil with salt and hot sauce. Cook for 3 to 5 minutes on high heat until cooked but al dente (still slightly crisp). Add Smoked Tomato Sauce, fusilli and spinach and heat through. Serve in pasta bowls garnished with a little grated Parmesan cheese.

Serves 6

For the tomato sauce: Cut tomatoes into quarters. Using a stovetop smoker or your barbecue, smoke tomatoes over high heat for 7 minutes. The wood chips can be placed on a piece of doubled-up aluminum foil fashioned roughly into a small tray. The foil is placed under the grill directly on the heat reflector of your propane burner.

In a medium-sized saucepan, sauté onion, garlic, celery, basil, oregano, chili flakes, salt and pepper in olive oil for 20 minutes over medium-low heat. Deglaze the pan with red wine and increase the heat, reducing the liquid by three-quarters. Add smoked tomatoes, sun-dried tomatoes, brown sugar and tomato juice and simmer for 1 hour.

The sauce can be puréed in a blender or mashed with a potato masher for a chunkier texture. (My preference is a smooth sauce for this particular pasta dish — the fusilli has edges that hold the sauce well.)

Serves 6 to 8

"Hodge Podge"

The quintessential hodge podge recipe doesn't exist. By that I mean I have never interviewed anyone who made it the same way as anyone else or tasted one that wasn't unique in some way. Some people use cream, some use only milk and some omit butter. The very best hodge podge recipes use baby vegetables and fresh garden peas, are properly seasoned and use butter.

1 lb (450 g) baby new potatoes, halved
8 oz (240 g) baby carrots
1 shallot, minced
2 cloves garlic, minced
¼ cup (60 mL) butter
¼ cup (60 mL) flour
4 cups (1 L) whole milk (4% m.f.)
8 oz (240 g) pattypan squash
4 oz (125 g) green beans
4 oz (125 g) yellow beans
4 oz (125 g) pearl onions
1 cup (250 mL) freshly shelled peas
2 sprigs fresh thyme
2 bay leaves
1 tsp (5 mL) salt
1 tsp (5 mL) freshly ground black pepper
1 cup (250 mL) heavy cream (35% m.f.)
¼ cup (60 mL) butter (second amount)
4 tbsp (60 mL) chopped chives

Blanch potatoes and carrots in a pot of salted water until tender but still firm. Drain and set aside.

In a second pot, sweat shallot and garlic in butter for 3 minutes. Add flour to make a roux and then pour cold milk slowly into the pot, whisking continuously. When sauce begins to thicken add all the vegetables, herbs and seasonings. Add cream and simmer for 1 hour or until vegetables are tender. Remove from heat and gently stir in the second amount of butter. Adjust salt and pepper to your personal taste.

Serve immediately, garnished with a few chopped chives.

Serves 6 to 8

Orecchiette Pasta with Montreal Proscuitto, Oven-dried Tomatoes, Creamed Globe Artichokes and Spinach

I developed this recipe for two reasons. First, globe artichokes are now grown in Nova Scotia's Gaspereau Valley. Second, I wanted to create a creamy "Alfredo" sauce that appeared to be rich and satisfying but was much healthier. This dish has just the right amount of "yum" with a fraction of the saturated fat. If you can't find fresh artichokes, use tinned ones, but watch how much extra salt you add.

Pasta

2 cups (500 mL) cooked orecchiette pasta
4 slices proscuitto, sliced into julienne strips
2 tbsp (30 mL) olive oil
1 shallot, minced
1 clove garlic, minced
4 tbsp (60 mL) dry sherry
2 cups (500 mL) Creamed Globe Artichokes (recipe follows)
6 Oven-dried Tomatoes (recipe follows)
2 cups (500 mL) cleaned organic spinach
½ cup (125 mL) Parmesan cheese
⅛ cup (60 mL) extra-virgin olive oil
freshly ground black pepper

Creamed Globe Artichokes

2 shallots, chopped
2 cloves garlic, chopped
2 cups (500 mL) chopped cooked fresh artichokes (see directions below)
3 cups (750 mL) vegetable stock
1 cup (250 mL) heavy cream (35% m.f.)
½ cup (125 mL) Parmesan cheese
1 tsp (5 mL) freshly ground black pepper
1 bay leaf
1 sprig fresh thyme
1 tsp (5 mL) dried oregano

Oven-dried Tomatoes

6 medium red tomatoes, cut in half through equator
1 tbsp (15 mL) white sugar
1 tsp (5 mL) salt
1 tsp (5 mL) freshly ground black pepper
1 tsp (5 mL) dried basil
1 tsp (5 mL) dried oregano

For the pasta: Cook orecchiette pasta, following instructions on the package.

Sauté proscuitto strips in oil with shallot and garlic for 2 minutes. Deglaze the pan with sherry and add Creamed Globe Artichokes, Oven-dried Tomatoes, orecchiette and spinach and heat through.

Serve in pasta bowls with grated Parmesan cheese, a drizzle of olive oil and fresh pepper.

Serves 4 to 6

For the fresh artichokes: Peel away the outer petals. Using a sharp knife, cut off the top 1 in (2.5 cm) or so. This will expose the inner "choke." Using a peeler, remove some of the outer stem as well as the woody bottom part of the vegetable.

Steam artichokes for 30 to 40 minutes in 1 in (2.5 cm) of water until they are soft. If any of the petals remain at all woody, remove them. Slice artichoke in half and use a small spoon to scoop out the hairy "choke" in the middle. You now have a fully cooked artichoke heart.

Combine all ingredients in a pot and simmer for 30 minutes. Purée and set aside.

Yields 6 cups (1.5 L). Leftovers freeze well.

For the oven-dried tomatoes: Place tomatoes, cut side up, on a baking rack. Mix dried spices together and sprinkle on top of the tomatoes. Bake overnight in a 100°F (40°C) oven.

Pumpkin Ravioli with Browned Butter, Aged Fig Vinegar, Walnut Cream and Chervil

This is a classic recipe for ravioli. In various parts of Italy, squash is combined with browned butter, Parmesan and balsamic vinegar. For the pasta you will need a pasta machine. If you do not have one, use wonton wrappers. They are a good substitute in a pinch. You don't have to look far to find locally grown pumpkin in the autumn.

Ravioli
3 cups (750 mL) peeled and diced pumpkin
4 tbsp (60 mL) olive oil
½ cup (125 mL) Parmesan cheese
2 egg yolks
½ tsp (3 mL) salt
½ tsp (3 mL) black pepper
Basic Pasta (see recipe in "Basics")

Browned butter
½ lb (225 g) salted butter

Walnut sauce
1 shallot
2 tbsp (30 mL) butter
½ tsp (3 mL) salt
½ tsp (3 mL) pepper
½ cup (125 mL) toasted chopped walnuts
4 tbsp (60 mL) brandy
⅛ tsp (1 mL) freshly grated nutmeg
1 ¼ cups (310 mL) heavy cream (35% m.f.)
⅓ cup (80 mL) Parmesan cheese
2 tbsp (30 mL) chopped chives
fig vinegar, for garnish
chervil leaves, for garnish

For the ravioli: Toss pumpkin in olive oil and roast in a 350°F (180°C) oven until golden and fully cooked. Place in a mixing bowl and mash well. When pumpkin is cool add remaining ingredients and mix to a smooth filling.

Using a pasta machine, roll out fresh pasta dough, following the manufacturer's instructions. Place each strip of pasta in a ravioli press and fill each pocket with pumpkin filling. Roll out a second sheet of pasta and brush with a little water. Place wet side down onto the filled sheet and press together. Unmould the ravioli and blanch in boiling salted water. When ravioli float they are ready to serve.

For the browned butter: Cook butter in a saucepan over medium heat. As it heats it will melt and eventually begin to foam. As the water evaporates, the milk solids will begin to brown. Stir with a wooden spoon, scraping the brown pieces off the bottom of the pan. When butter is a light, nutty brown colour remove from the heat and set aside. The butter will continue to brown in the pan, especially if you are using a high-quality, thick-bottomed pan that retains a lot of heat. To ensure a perfect brown butter, pour into a cool bowl once it reaches the desired colour.

For the walnut sauce: Sauté shallots for 3 minutes in butter and add salt, pepper and walnuts. Cook over medium-high heat for 2 minutes and deglaze the pan with brandy. Be careful as the brandy will flame as it heats up. Add nutmeg and cream and reduce sauce by one-third or until it thickens slightly. Add cheese and chives and toss ravioli in sauce just prior to serving.

Serve about 7 ravioli per person. Drizzle about 1 tablespoon of fig vinegar and 2 tablespoons of brown butter over each plate. Garnish with chervil leaves and some additional grated Parmesan if desired.

Serves 4 to 6

Four-cheese Gnocchi

In the north of Italy, potato gnocchi is soft and smooth and melts in the mouth. Further to the south the gnocchi is firmer and has an *al dente* texture like the pasta. Each has its own characteristics and works well in different dishes. However, since my trip to Torino in 2006, gnocchi for me has meant the former. Served in a rich and wonderful cheese sauce, when properly made this dish is absolutely amazing. It is the essence of Italian cooking for me — simplicity and tradition, executed perfectly. Local cheeses can also be used despite the distinct Italian heritage to this dish. Try a Quebec blue instead of Gorgonzola, a 6-year aged cheddar instead of Romano, and a mild brie for the provolone.

Gnocchi

2 lb (1 kg) russet potatoes
4 egg yolks
1 tsp (5 mL) salt
¼ tsp (2 mL) pepper
1 ½ cups (375 mL) flour

Cheese sauce

1 shallot, minced
1 clove garlic, minced
2 tbsp (30 mL) butter
2 tbsp (30 mL) flour
½ tsp (3 mL) salt
¼ cup (60 mL) white wine
2 cups (500 mL) milk (2% m.f. or whole)
1 ½ cups (375 mL) heavy cream (35% m.f.)
¼ tsp (3 mL) freshly grated nutmeg
3 drops Tabasco or other hot sauce
⅛ cup (35 mL) grated Parmesan
½ cup (125 mL) grated Romano
½ cup (125 mL) grated provolone
¼ cup (80 mL) crumbled Gorgonzola

For the gnocchi: Bake potatoes in a 400°F (200°C) oven for 1 hour. Cut in half and scoop out flesh, discarding the skins. If available, rice the potatoes in a potato ricer or food mill. If not, mash with a fork. Allow to cool. Combine egg yolks, salt and pepper in a small bowl and whisk together. Add to cooled potatoes and mix thoroughly. Combine flour with potatoes and knead only until a dough forms. Divide dough into 4 small balls and roll each ball into a long snake-shaped string about ½ in (12 mm) in diameter. Using a knife cut into ¾-in (2-cm) pieces.

At this point you can place the gnocchi on a tray and freeze individually for later use. To continue making this recipe, bring a pot of salted water to the boil and set gnocchi to one side.

For the cheese sauce: Gently cook shallot and garlic in butter for 5 minutes until translucent. Add flour to form a roux, and salt. Cook over medium heat for 3 minutes. Add wine and whisk until a smooth paste forms. While whisking continuously add milk and bring to a simmer. Add cream and continue to simmer the sauce for 10 minutes on low heat. Add nutmeg, hot sauce and four cheeses and stir until melted and smooth.

Drop gnocchi into boiling water and cook for 3 to 5 minutes. They will float when they are ready. Add gnocchi to the cheese sauce and serve immediately in a pasta or soup bowl, garnished with fresh herbs or grated Parmesan cheese.

Serves 8

Root Vegetable Tart

Unlike a gratin, which is generally saucy and needs to be scooped out of a deep dish casserole, this tart is firmer and can be cut and served like a piece of pie. It is particularly good with turkey, chicken or pork loin, as the sage and cranberry element is an obvious match. The preparation of the vegetables is the key to success here.

1 small turnip (about 1 ¼ lb/675 g)
2 sweet potatoes
1 medium-sized celery root
4 parsnips
4 carrots
½ lb (225 g) salted butter
2 cups (500 mL) cranberries
1 cup (250 mL) minced onion
¼ cup (60 mL) chicken, beef or vegetable stock
2 tbsp (30 mL) salt
freshly ground black pepper
¼ cup (60 mL) chopped fresh sage

Peel all the vegetables and slice into large rounds or ovals about ⅛-in (2-mm) thick. A mandoline works best but a sharp knife is effective. Line a casserole dish with a piece of parchment paper cut to fit exactly into the bottom. Rub paper liberally with butter. Layer vegetables, beginning with the largest pieces of sweet potato. This will be the top of the tart when it is flipped out of the pan and the orange colour will be visible. Alternate types of vegetables, but in two of the layers add cranberries and minced onions along with a drizzle of stock. Season each layer with salt, pepper and a little fresh sage, and place a few dollops of butter in with the seasonings. The last layer of the tart, which will be the eventual bottom, should be turnip. These slices are larger and will give the tart stability when plated.

Set another piece of buttered parchment on the top. Using another casserole dish, slightly smaller than the first, weight the tart and place in a 350°F (180°C) for 1 hour. At this point remove the second casserole dish and parchment and return to the oven for another hour. When a knife goes through the centre with ease, remove from the oven and allow to cool. Unmould the tart carefully onto a cutting board and slice into pieces 3 in (7.5 cm) square. Each can be reheated in the oven or microwave before serving.

Serves 6, with leftovers

King Crab and Mascarpone Risotto

Every now and then a group of friends and I gather for a full Sunday of cooking. Usually we have hobby chefs coming through my good friend John Corney's kitchen all day long, drinking wine and tasting a new dish. John is very particular about his food and is very hard to please. One day we made more than 13 dishes, and even John was impressed with this winner of a risotto. We used fresh crab just caught near Cheticamp, Cape Breton.

2 shallots, minced
1 clove garlic, minced
¼ bulb anise, minced
¼ cup (60 mL) butter
½ tsp (3 mL) freshly ground black pepper
1 cup (250 mL) Italian Arborio or Caranoli rice
½ cup (125 mL) dry vermouth
3 cups (750 mL) low-sodium chicken broth
1 cup (250 mL clam juice
2 cups (500 mL) cooked and chunked king crab meat
1 cup (250 mL) mascarpone cheese
4 tbsp (60 mL) fresh chervil leaves

Sauté shallots, garlic and anise in butter over medium heat for 10 minutes until soft and translucent. Add pepper and rice and stir well to coat in fat. Cook for 3 minutes until rice looks translucent. In a separate pot, bring chicken broth and clam juice to a boil. Add vermouth and cook out liquid completely before adding hot broth and clam juice, one ladle at a time until liquid is fully incorporated. The rice will take about 15 to 18 minutes to cook, depending on the variety. Add crab and mascarpone cheese and just heat through. For a soupier risotto it may be necessary to add another ½ cup (125 mL) of chicken stock at the end. Adjust salt to taste as many commercially available stocks and clam juice products have a high sodium content.

Serve in soup bowls, garnished with a few leaves of fresh chervil.

Serves 6

Roast Garlic and Cremini Mushroom Pappardelle with Roast Chicken

This is a fantastic dish if you have leftover roast chicken in your refrigerator. It is also a simple way to stretch one of those small roasted chicken available at so many supermarkets these days. Cremini mushrooms are grown locally year-round, but the dish is so warm and rich it is perfect for colder evening meals. The mushrooms are prepared in two ways — both as a base for the sauce and also sautéed in the pasta. The essential ingredient here is the roasted garlic. Roasting brings out the sweet sugars and makes the dish balance better than raw garlic. The inspiration for the pasta is chicken tetrazzini, but I like this version, as it uses less cream and is better for you.

2 heads garlic
1 tbsp (15 mL) olive oil
½ cup (125 mL) dried porcini mushrooms
½ cup (125 mL) sherry
1 medium onion, diced
1 stalk celery, chopped
½ cup (125 mL) extra-virgin olive oil
2 tbsp (30 mL) fresh thyme leaves
1 ½ lb (675 g) whole cremini mushrooms
1 tsp (5 mL) salt
1 tsp (5 mL) pepper
4 cups (1 L) chicken stock
1 cup (250 mL) heavy cream (35% m.f.)
2 tbsp (30 mL) olive oil (second amount)
1 lb (450 g) cremini mushrooms (second amount), sliced
1 small roasted chicken, meat picked and shredded by hand
1 lb (450 g) cooked pappardelle pasta
¼ cup (80 mL) chopped Italian parsley
¼ cup (80 mL) grated Pecorino Romano cheese

Rub olive oil over the skin of garlic heads and roast in a 300°F (150°C) oven for 1 hour. When cool to the touch, use a serrated knife and cut about ¼ in (5 mm) off the root end of the bulb. Squeeze out cloves into a bowl, mash with a fork and set aside.

In a small bowl, soak dried porcini mushrooms in sherry until hydrated and soft, about 1 hour.

In a large saucepan, cook onion, celery, olive oil, thyme, whole cremini mushrooms, salt and pepper over medium heat for 30 minutes. Deglaze the pan with sherry and hydrated mushrooms. Add chicken stock and simmer for 30 minutes. Purée in a blender and strain through a chinois or fine-meshed strainer. Add cream and set sauce aside.

In a large nonstick sauté pan, heat olive oil and sauté sliced cremini mushrooms until slightly golden brown. Add puréed sauce and shredded chicken meat and heat only until the meat is warmed through, about 3 to 5 minutes.

To serve, ladle sauce over cooked pappardelle pasta. Garnish with chopped parsley and Pecorino Romano cheese.

Serves 8 to 10

Smoked Bacon, Oka Cheese and Sweet Potato Gratin

I make this for my mother every Christmas. I never follow a recipe so this one I tested recently and it worked very well, especially with the fantastic Oka cheese. Its flavour is much like a Swiss Alpenzeller or Gruyère: pleasingly nutty and full of robust earthy aroma. The casserole goes very well with a turkey dinner and is even better next day with the leftovers!

1 cup (250 mL) diced onion
2 cloves garlic
6 slices smoky bacon, minced
1 tbsp (15 mL) olive oil
1 cup (250 mL) chicken broth
½ cup (125 mL) heavy cream (35% m.f.)
2 lb (1 kg) peeled sweet potato, in lengthwise slices, 1/8-in (2-mm) thick
1 ½ cups (375 mL) Canadian Oka cheese
4 tbsp (60 mL) butter
1 cup (250 mL) breadcrumbs

In a saucepan, sauté onion, garlic and bacon in oil until the onions are slightly browned.

In a separate pot, bring chicken broth and cream to a boil. Set aside.

Grease a casserole dish with a little butter or oil and layer it with sliced sweet potatoes. After each layer sprinkle some bacon and onion mixture and a little cheese. Moisten each layer with 2 tablespoons of chicken broth and cream. Repeat the layering until the potatoes are about ½ in (12 mm) from the top. In a separate frying pan, melt butter and combine with breadcrumbs. Sprinkle this mixture over potatoes.

Place casserole dish in a 350°F (180°C) oven for about 1 hour. Do not cover. If breadcrumbs become too dark simply lower the oven temperature to 300°F (150°C) and continue cooking until a knife is easily inserted through the sweet potatoes.

Serves 4

Baked Beans with Ham Hocks

Like so many Nova Scotians, I grew up having beans as Saturday supper. It is still a great treat to have them, particularly at brunch. Many great family restaurants in the Maritimes serve beans with fish cakes, another classic. I have chosen to keep this recipe simple in the spirit of the country dish but have added a smoked ham hock instead of pork fat for a more complete meal. For a vegetarian option, simply omit the ham hock and proceed as normal in the recipe.

1 large smoked ham hock (approximately 1 ¼ lb/600 g)
2 lb (1 kg) dried white navy beans, soaked overnight in water
   (water discarded)
1 tbsp (15 mL) dry mustard
⅔ cup (160 mL) brown sugar
½ cup (125 mL) molasses
2 tsp (10 mL) salt
1 tsp (5 mL) pepper
2 medium onions studded with 6 whole cloves
2 bay leaves

Score ham hock with a paring knife in 3 or 4 places. Then simply combine all ingredients in a covered earthenware dish. Cover with water, ½ in (12 mm) above the level of the beans. Bake at 300 °F (150°C) for 6 to 8 hours. Check beans regularly and add boiling water if necessary to keep them moist. When beans are fully cooked, remove ham hock and allow to cool so it can be handled. Remove fat and pick meat off the bone, shredding it into small pieces. Add meat back to beans and serve with brown bread and butter.

Serves 8 to 10

Walnut Blue Cheese Risotto

I serve this risotto with Dried Fruit-stuffed Pork Loin (page 128). The idea for the dish came from a simple cheese plate: blue cheese, nuts, port wine and fruit. Make sure you use a quality blue like Gorgonzola, Stilton or a local artisan cheese. I always use a well-known Nova Scotia-made cheese called Dragon's Breath Blue. It is wonderfully creamy and the musty flavour is just enough to hold up against the flavours of the roast pork and stewed fruit.

3 shallots, minced
1 stalk celery, minced
4 tbsp (60 mL) butter
2 tbsp (30 mL) olive oil
1 tsp (5 mL) salt
1 tsp (5 mL) pepper
1 cup (250 mL) Italian Arborio or Caranoli rice
½ cup (125 mL) port wine
3 ½ cups (875 mL) low-sodium chicken broth, heated
1 cup (250 mL) toasted walnut halves
¾ cup (180 mL) crumbled blue cheese
1 tbsp (15 mL) toasted walnut oil
2 tbsp (30 mL) chopped chives

Sauté shallots and celery in butter and oil until soft. Add rice and cook for 3 minutes on medium heat until grains look translucent. Deglaze the pan with port wine and cook until the bottom of the pan is dry. Begin adding hot stock 1 cup (250 mL) at a time, stirring constantly. The risotto will take about 15 to 18 minutes to cook, depending on the variety of rice. When the risotto is fully cooked but still al dente (the grain still gives some resistance when bitten) remove from the heat and stir in walnut halves, blue cheese and walnut oil.

Serve garnished with chopped chives.

Serves 4 to 6

Fish

So many seafood dishes are deeply rooted in our Canadian culture. We have all enjoyed a delicious piece of fried fish with new potatoes and garden greens or a fishcake with baked beans and tartar sauce at one time or another.

In Nova Scotia, where I am from, seafood is precious. For some people, items like lobster, scallops and oysters are luxuries to be enjoyed only on special occasions. For others, they provide a necessary source of income — fishing has been a way of life for generations of Maritime families.

The once-abundant, but now decimated, codfish is the ultimate example of how our food traditions, as well as our cultural ones, are tied so strongly to the natural world around us. And as debates about sustainable fisheries and farmed salmon rage on in all parts of Canada, they are having a great impact on the choices that environmentally concerned chefs are making when they build their menus.

Fish and seafood are one of the most dynamic areas of our food supply. Their availability will always be at the mercy of the tides and the ever-changing seasons. If a fisherman hasn't caught it, you can't have it, unless it is cultivated on a fish farm. This means that to cook successfully with seafood we must procure the very best that nature allows us and then use our creativity.

I hope to show a new level of respect for the jewels of the sea in this chapter. This respect comes from my desire to not only cook the very finest fish and seafood, but also to do so in a way that will allow future generations to share in the wealth of Canada's oceans.

Grilled Lobster with Aged Balsamic-glazed Fiddleheads and Jerusalem Artichoke Purée

Lobster can be grilled in the shell or on a skewer. If you are grilling it in the shell it must be cut in half while still alive, a task that some cooks find unpleasant. If your local fishmonger sells shelled raw tail and claw meat it will work well here. Jerusalem artichokes are a little uncommon in home kitchens but with their rich and buttery flavour they make a nice potato-like accompaniment to this lobster dish. They can be found at organic markets, your local farmers' market, and once in a while, at the grocery store.

Artichoke purée
1 ½ cups (375 mL) well-cleaned Jerusalem artichokes
½ cup (125 mL) peeled and chopped potato
½ cup (125 mL) milk
3 tbsp (45 mL) butter
½ tsp (3 mL) salt
½ tsp (3 mL) pepper

Fiddleheads
1 ½ cups (375 mL) fresh fiddleheads
¼ cup (60 mL) water
⅛ tsp (1 mL) salt
2 tbsp (30 mL) salted butter
⅛ tsp (1 mL) freshly ground black pepper
2 tbsp (30 mL) aged balsamic vinegar (aged 10 to 12 years minimum)

Grilled lobster
1 tbsp (15 mL) minced shallot
1 tsp (5 mL) minced garlic
1 tsp (5 mL) freshly grated ginger
juice and zest of ½ lemon
¼ tsp (1 mL) ground fennel seeds
½ tsp (3 mL) white sugar
1 drop Tabasco sauce
2 tbsp (30 mL) extra-virgin olive oil
¼ tsp (1 mL) sea salt
4 lobster tails, shells removed and deveined
4 lobster claws

For the artichoke purée: Coarsely chop Jerusalem artichokes. Use a stainless steel pot to prevent discolouring the artichokes. The milk will also help keep the colour creamy-white. Combine all ingredients in the pot and simmer, covered, for 30 minutes. Place mixture in a food processor and purée until smooth.

For the fiddleheads: Steam fiddleheads in salted water for 6 minutes in a covered saucepan. Pour off all excess water and add butter. Sauté for 3 minutes over medium heat and season with pepper and vinegar.

For the lobster: Combine all ingredients except lobster in a bowl and whisk to form a marinade. Toss lobster meat in marinade and skewer, with one tail and one claw per skewer. The skewer can be inserted through the tail lengthwise to prevent the meat from curling up on the grill. Allow meat to marinate for one hour before grilling. Preheat barbecue to high and clean the surface well. Grill lobster for 2 minutes on each side and carefully slide off the skewer just prior to serving. Season with a little sea salt, if desired.

Serve the lobster on top of a small pile of artichoke purée surrounded by the fiddleheads. Please note, this recipe can be done very much the same way using in-shell lobster. Simply cut the lobster in half and grill for an extra 2 minutes per side.

Serves 4

Whole Poached Salmon with Poached Free-range Egg, Pickled Asparagus and Chive Beurre Blanc

This dish was designed to utilize the whole fish and was inspired by the way my mother used to make salmon when I was a kid. Wrapped in cheesecloth and poached, the flesh was scooped out with a spoon and dressed with a white béchamel sauce garnished with chopped boiled egg.

Whole poached salmon

1 medium onion, quartered
2 stalks celery
4 bay leaves
4 sprigs fresh thyme
1 cup white wine
1 tbsp cracked black peppercorns
1 ½ gallons (6 L) water
1 x 6-lb (2 ½-kg) whole salmon, drawn and well cleaned
1 lemon, sliced
1 bunch parsley
1 package cheesecloth (or a 6-ft length)
6 free-range eggs (or 1 per person)
1 Pickled Asparagus (see recipe in "Pickles and Preserves" chapter)
1 cup Chive Beurre Blanc Sauce (recipe follows)

Chive beurre blanc sauce

1 shallot, finely chopped
¼ cup (60 mL) white wine
juice of ½ lemon
1 tsp (5 mL) white wine vinegar
1 tbsp (15 mL) whipping cream (35% m.f.)
¾ cup (180 mL) cold butter, cut into ½-in (1-cm) cubes
2 drops Tabasco sauce
2 tbsp (30 mL) chopped chives

For the fish: Choose a pot with a diameter roughly the same as the total length of the salmon. Special poaching pans for whole fish are available, but not many home cooks have one. Place onion, celery, bay leaves, thyme, wine, peppercorns and water in the pot and bring to a boil. Reduce the heat to a simmer or a poaching temperature of 130°F (55°C).

Clean salmon well and stuff the belly cavity with lemon slices and parsley. Pack it in as well as you can and then wrap salmon in cheesecloth. Tie each end with a piece of string and set into the poaching liquid. Poach for about 20 minutes, or until an internal thermometer reads 130°F (55°C). Gently lift salmon from the pot by the strings on each end and rest on a tray.

With the heat still under the pot of poaching liquid, crack eggs into the pot and poach for 4 minutes.

To assemble, cut open cheesecloth with a pair of scissors and peel back salmon skin. The meat will lift away from the bones easily with the use of a spoon. Serve about 8 oz (225 g) per person. Place 3 spears of Pickled Asparagus on each salmon portion, followed by one poached egg. Pour 2 or 3 tablespoons of Chive Beurre Blanc Sauce over each and serve immediately.

Serves 6 to 10, depending on size of salmon

For the beurre blanc sauce: Place shallot, white wine, lemon juice and vinegar in a saucepan and bring to a boil. Reduce the liquid to 2 tablespoons total. Add whipping cream and just bring to a boil. Remove from heat and begin whisking cold butter into the reduction a little (about 4 cubes) at a time. As the butter melts and incorporates into the reduction the sauce will thicken. It may be necessary to put the pot back over the heat for a few seconds now and then. When all the butter is incorporated, season the sauce with Tabasco and add chives. If you used salted butter no extra salt will be needed; if you used unsalted butter, season to taste.

Yields 1 cup (250 mL)

Proscuitto-wrapped Monkfish with Chard and Cape Breton Mustard Pickles

It may be ugly in appearance but monkfish, or anglerfish, contains meat that is far from ugly. Sometimes called "poor man's lobster," the meat is sweet and firm. It sears and grills well because it is easy to handle. The Mustard Pickles make a perfect tangy match to the sweet fish and the salty prosciutto wrap.

4 monkfish tail pieces, bone out (about 6 to 8 oz/180 to 240 g each)
several grindings of fresh black pepper
4 thin slices prosciutto
2 tbsp (30 mL) extra-virgin olive oil
2 tbsp butter
1 shallot, minced
1 lb (450 g) Swiss chard, cleaned and stems removed
1 cup (250 mL) Mustard Pickles (see recipe in "Pickles and Preserves" chapter)

Ask your fishmonger to remove the thin membrane on the outside of the tail. If you purchase frozen fish you must do this yourself at home. Simply pierce the membrane with a sharp paring knife and carefully cut it away without removing too much of the white flesh underneath. Cut tails in half, making 8 portions. Season with a little pepper.

Cut prosciutto in half lengthwise, making 8 long, thin slices. Wrap each piece of monkfish with a piece of prosciutto (like a napkin ring). Heat a nonstick frying pan to medium and sear wrapped monkfish in olive oil on all sides. Remove from the frying pan and complete the cooking in a 300°F (150°C) oven for 8 minutes.

In the same pan you used to sear the fish, add butter and cook shallot for 3 minutes. Do not add any salt, as the oil remaining in the pan from the prosciutto will be salty. Add Swiss chard and cook until it is fully wilted. Add a little more pepper if desired and serve immediately.

To serve, pile Swiss chard in the middle of a plate. Place fish on top (one piece per plate for an appetizer, two for an entree) and garnish with a heaping spoonful of Mustard Pickles. Accompany with boiled new potatoes.

Serves 4 as a main, 8 as an appetizer

Cedar-planked Sea Trout with Hodge Podge

Planked salmon is a staple on restaurant menus throughout Atlantic Canada and at barbecues during the summer. I simply like the flavour and texture of sea trout and the fact that the fillets are smaller — they cook faster, without becoming over-smoked and acidic. Fresh basil, straight from the herb garden, complements the fish perfectly.

2 cedar planks
2 sea trout fillets, bones removed, skin on
1 lemon
1 lime
½ cup (125 mL) fresh basil leaves
1 tsp (5 mL) fleur de sel
1 tsp (5 mL) freshly ground black pepper
1 spray bottle of water
Hodge Podge (see recipe in "Pasta, Risotto and Side Dishes" chapter)

Soak cedar planks in water for several hours before cooking. Place 1 trout on each plank, skin side down, flesh side up. The skin insulates the fish during cooking and keeps it moist. Thinly slice lemon and lime and place alternate slices in a single line down the centre of each fillet. Tuck basil leaves between each slice and over the fish, but do not completely cover the flesh.

Preheat barbecue to medium/high and place planks on the grill. Cover and remain close by with a spray bottle of water in case there is a flare-up. Cook for about 8 to 12 minutes, depending on the barbecue and thickness of the fillet. The fish should be medium in the middle or still slightly orange.

To serve, carefully scoop the fish from the plank, sliding a spatula between the meat and the skin. Usually the skin will stick to the wood. Remove the lemons, limes and basil leaves and season with a little fleur de sel and pepper. Serve on top of creamy Hodge Podge with brown bread, butter and, of course, Mustard Pickles (see recipe in "Pickles and Preserves" chapter).

Serves 6 to 8

Basil Pesto Crusted Sea Bass with Charred Cherry Tomatoes and Pine Nuts

This dish exemplifies how simple ingredients served at the peak of freshness can stand alone and, indeed, rise above complicated and pretentious dishes. I also like making Basil Pesto when the herb is flourishing in the garden and freezing it in small plastic tubs. It thaws in an hour or so and can add a bright garden-fresh taste even after the herb beds are bare.

Fish
- 2 x 8-oz (225-g) sea bass fillets, skin on
- 2 tbsp (30 mL) Basil Pesto (recipe follows)
- 1 tsp (5 mL) canola oil
- 1 ½ cups (375 mL) mixed-colour cherry tomatoes
- ½ cup (125 mL) fresh basil leaves
- 4 tbsp (60 mL) toasted pine nuts
- 4 tbsp (60 mL) extra-virgin olive oil
- ¼ tsp (1 mL) sea salt
- ¼ tsp (1 mL) freshly ground black pepper

Basil pesto
- 2 cups (500 mL) packed fresh basil leaves
- 2 cloves garlic, cut in half with germ removed
- ¼ cup (60 mL) toasted pine nuts
- ¼ cup (60 mL) extra-virgin olive oil
- ¼ cup (60 mL) grated Parmesan cheese
- salt and pepper to taste

For the fish: Using a knife, make 3 incisions in the skin of the sea bass, about ¼ inch (5 mm) deep. This is easily done by gently "pinching" the fillet between your thumb and index finger to create tension in the muscle. These cuts prevent the fillet from curling up during roasting. On the flesh side of each fillet spread 1 tbsp (15 mL) of Basil Pesto.

Preheat oven to 400°F (200°C). Rub 1 tsp (5 mL) of canola oil into the cooking surface of a cast iron pan, using a paper towel. Heat the pan over a hot burner until it begins to smoke. Place sea bass in the centre of the pan, skin side down, and add cherry tomatoes around the fish. Place pan in the oven and roast for 5 minutes. Remove from oven and toss in basil leaves, pine nuts, olive oil, salt and pepper.

Serve immediately.

Serves 2

For the pesto: Place basil leaves, garlic and pine nuts in a food processor and pulse until coarsely chopped. Switch processor to high and add olive oil in a steady stream through the top of the lid. Occasionally remove the top and scrape the mixture down from the sides. When the pesto is smooth stir in Parmesan cheese and seasonings.

Potato-crusted Cod, Browned Butter Celery Root Purée and Muscat-braised Summer Leeks

Encrusting fish in potato is difficult without the right tools, but Asian food markets often have vegetable peelers that produce ribbons as required in this recipe. An apple peeler can also be used. One way to achieve a similar effect is to bread the fish in dehydrated potato using a flour-and-egg dredging procedure. When choosing fresh fish fillets remember that they should smell only of the ocean, have a lovely shiny flesh, and be stored on shaved ice at the fishmonger's.

Fish
2 cups (500 mL) vegetable oil
4 x 4-oz (120-g) portions fresh cod fillets
½ tsp (2 mL) sea salt
½ tsp (2 mL) pepper
4 tbsp (60 mL) potato flour
2 Yukon gold potatoes, peeled
½ tsp (2 mL) fleur de sel

Celery root purée
1 medium celery root, peeled and coarsely chopped
1 tsp (5 mL) salt
½ cup (125 mL) salted butter
½ tsp (3 mL) Tabasco sauce
1 tsp (5 mL) lemon juice

Braised leeks
4 small summer leeks cut into 3-in (7.5-cm) lengths
1 cup Muscat wine
1 tbsp (15 mL) butter
⅛ tsp (1 mL) salt
a grinding of fresh black pepper

For the cod: Preheat vegetable oil in a steep-sided saucepan until it reaches 350°F (180°C), using a fry thermometer. Season each fillet with salt and pepper on both sides and lightly dredge in potato flour. Using an upright, table-mounted apple peeler, place peeled potatoes in the machine and turn the handle continuously until the potato is completely shredded. Remove the top and grab the end of the potato ribbon. Wrap at least two layers of potato ribbon around the fillets and tuck the final strand underneath the end where the first strands of potato were wrapped around the fish. This is to prevent unravelling in the frying fat. Fry each fillet in the oil for about 4 minutes or until golden brown. Remove from oil and place on a paper towel to remove any excess grease.

Sprinkle a small amount of fleur de sel on each fillet just before serving.

For the celery root purée: Steam celery root in 2 cups (500 mL) salted water for 20 minutes or until very soft. Drain and place celery root in a food processor. In a small saucepan, cook butter over medium heat. As the butter cooks it will foam up and milk solids will begin to brown on the bottom of the pan. Use a wooden spoon and continuously scrape milk solids from the bottom of the pan. The butter will turn a light brown colour and develop a nutty aroma. Pour butter over the cooked celery root in the food processor and add Tabasco sauce and lemon juice. Process on high for 3 minutes until mixture is velvety smooth.

For the Muscat-braised leeks: Place all ingredients in a small saucepan and simmer, covered, for 20 minutes on low heat. Remove leeks from pan and reduce remaining liquid by three-quarters. Add leeks back to the pan and toss in the reduction.

Serve the dish by spooning celery root purée and leeks onto the centre of a warm dinner plate. Place the crispy fish on top and garnish as desired.

Serves 4

Bouillabaisse with Aioli

Bouillabaisse is fish stew. The two essential ingredients (besides the freshest seafood you can possibly get your hands on) are tomatoes and saffron. My recipe is a more modern version than the simple and hearty French soup of Provence. I make a clear consommé broth from perfectly ripe tomatoes and season it with oyster liquor and saffron. The fish is then gently poached just prior to serving in the aromatic broth. The traditional accompaniment here is aioli and crusty French bread.

Keep in mind when making this dish that every time it was made in the old days it was different, as it relied on what was brought ashore that day at the wharf. Don't get too caught up in the type of seafood — only be concerned with buying the freshest possible.

Broth (consommé)
4 lb (1.8 kg) ripe red tomatoes, quartered
½ anise bulb, coarsely chopped
3 shallots, coarsely chopped
3 cloves garlic, coarsely chopped
½ cup (125 mL) white wine
1 tbsp (15 mL) white sugar
1 cup (250 mL) clam juice
1 tsp Tabasco sauce
¼ cup (60 mL) fresh basil
1 large sheet cheesecloth (1 package)

Bouillabaisse
1 tsp (5 mL) saffron
12 medium-sized choice oysters, shucked and liquor reserved
1 lb (450 g) fresh scallops
1 lb (450 g) cleaned mussels
2 lb (900 g) pasta clams or quahogs
2 lb (450 g) snow crab legs
1 lb (450 g) fresh Arctic char or salmon fillet
1 lb (450 g) halibut, hake or tilapia fillet, optional
1 lb (450 g) smelts, optional
meat from 1 cooked lobster, optional
1 cup (250 mL) ripe cherry tomatoes
Aioli (see recipe in "Basics" chapter)

For the consommé: Combine all ingredients (not the cheesecloth) in a pot and simmer for 30 minutes. Remove from stove and allow to cool until just warm. Line a large mixing bowl with squares of cut cheesecloth. You will need plenty of slack over the sides of the bowl and at least 5 layers of cloth. Carefully pour the contents of the pot into the bowl. Gather the slack ends of cheesecloth over the top of the mix and tie shut with a piece of butcher's twine (this is the same process used in making apple jelly). Hang the mixture from a shelf in your fridge with a clean bowl under it for at least 12 hours. The liquid released will be a clear but flavourful tomato nectar.

For the bouillabaisse: Gently reheat tomato consommé in a large pot and add saffron and reserved liquor from the oysters. Simmer for 10 minutes and then add the seafood. If you have quahogs you may have to add them first as they take a bit longer than everything else. When the shells have popped open on all the shellfish and the scallops are just cooked, the soup is ready.

Serve immediately while the seafood is perfectly warmed through and garnish with sliced cherry tomatoes and a heaping spoonful of aioli.

Serves 6

Olive Oil–poached Halibut with Puttanesca Summer Squash

Poaching fish in oil sounds like it would add unnecessary calories to an otherwise healthy dish. If done properly, however, the fish soaks up very little oil and only the beautiful flavour. Poaching also keeps moisture in the meat. To cook it right you will need a thermometer and individually portioned, thick fillets of halibut, free of skin and bones.

4 cups (1 L) olive oil
1 shallot
2 cloves garlic, cut in half
4 bay leaves
1 sprig fresh rosemary
2 sprigs fresh thyme
zest of 1 lemon
1 tsp (5 mL) freshly cracked black peppercorns
1 tsp (5 mL) cracked coriander seeds
4 x 8-oz (200-g) portions skinless, boneless halibut, at least 1in
  (2.5 cm) thick
fleur de sel for garnishing
Puttanesca Summer Squash (see recipe in "Vegetarian Dishes"
  chapter)

In a small deep-sided saucepan, heat olive oil and all ingredients except halibut portions to 200°F (100°C), and hold there for 30 minutes. Reduce the heat. When the temperature reaches 145°F (65°C), add halibut. The oil must cover each piece of fish completely. If it does not, try using a smaller-diameter saucepan. Poach fish for 8 minutes or until the internal temperature reads 140 to 145°F (60 to 65°C). Remove from oil and season with a little fleur de sel or good-quality sea salt.

Serve halibut with Puttanesca Summer Squash.

Serves 4

Smoked Line-caught Haddock Cakes with Sweet Corn and Tartar Sauce

This is no ordinary fishcake and no ordinary tartar sauce. The smoky haddock and sweet corn work perfectly together and the crunchy and slightly acidic condiment finish it off beautifully. I smoke my own fresh haddock and purchase line-caught whenever possible. However, there are many very good smokehouses that make a great smoked haddock, so pick some up if you can. Smoked mackerel or hot-smoked salmon make very good substitutes here.

Fishcakes

4 tbsp (60 mL) minced red onion
4 tbsp (60 mL) minced celery
4 tbsp (60 mL) minced red pepper
1 clove garlic, minced
1 cup (250 mL) fresh kernel corn
3 tbsp (45 mL) salted butter
1 tsp (5 mL) salt
1 ½ lb (675 g) smoked haddock
1 medium potato, cooked and grated
½ cup (125 mL) fresh breadcrumbs
1 cup (250 mL) mayonnaise
1 tsp (5 mL) Tabasco or hot sauce
1 tsp (5 mL) Worcestershire sauce
2 tbsp (30 mL) chopped green onion tops or chives

Breading

3 eggs
¼ tsp (1 mL) salt
¼ tsp (1 mL) pepper
½ cup (125 mL) flour
1 ½ cups (375 mL) panko or regular dried breadcrumbs
¼ cup (60 mL) vegetable oil

Tartar sauce

3 tbsp (45 mL) minced Pickled Red Onions (see recipe in "Pickles and Preserves" chapter), or fresh red onion
2 tbsp (30 mL) finely chopped capers
¼ cup (60 mL) diced gherkins
1 tbsp (30 mL) sweet green relish
1 cup (250 mL) mayonnaise
¼ cup (60 mL) sour cream
1 tsp (5 mL) Tabasco sauce
1 tsp (5 mL) Worcestershire sauce
juice and zest of 1 lemon
½ tsp (2 mL) salt
¼ tsp (1 mL) freshly ground black pepper
2 tbsp (30 mL) chopped chives, optional

For the fishcakes: Sweat red onion, celery, red pepper, garlic and corn in butter and salt until onions are translucent. In a large mixing bowl, flake haddock into small pieces using your fingers. Add grated potato, fresh breadcrumbs, sweated vegetables, mayonnaise, Tabasco sauce, Worcestershire sauce and green onions and mix thoroughly using your hands. Form into 5-oz (140-g) cakes and chill in refrigerator for a minimum of 1 hour before breading.

For the breading: In a small mixing bowl, beat eggs with salt and pepper. Dredge fishcakes first in flour, then eggwash and finally breadcrumbs. Heat vegetable oil in a nonstick frying pan and fry breaded fishcakes over medium heat until crisp and golden, about 6 minutes per side.

For the tartar sauce: Combine all ingredients in a small mixing bowl and stir well to incorporate.

Store in a sealed container, refrigerated, for up to 10 days.

Simply serve 2 cakes with a heaping spoonful of tartar sauce and garnish with herbs or microgreens.

Serves 8 as an appetizer or 4 as an entrée

Roast Wild Salmon with Colcannon and Green Tomato Chow

Salmon, potatoes, greens and chow scream Maritime cooking to me. Notice how the oven temperature is lowered and the skin is left on the salmon during cooking. Both these measures ensure that the fish will retain its moisture content as it roasts. I had colcannon for the first time in 1994 when I was backpacking around Ireland. It was served with fried salmon at a small pub, and I have been hooked ever since.

Colcannon

1 ½ lb (675 g) yellow-fleshed potatoes, unpeeled and quartered
1 tsp (5 mL) salt
8 oz (225 g) washed green kale, coarsely chopped
1 tsp pepper
½ cup (125mL) salted butter
¼ cup (60 mL) thinly sliced green onion tops

Fish

2 tbsp (30 mL) vegetable oil
6 x 6-oz (170-g) salmon fillets, skin on, bones removed
¼ tsp (1 mL) salt
¼ tsp (2 mL) pepper
4 tbsp (60 mL) butter
1 cup (250 mL) Green Tomato Chow (see recipe in "Pickles and Preserves" chapter)

For the colcannon: Boil potatoes in salted water for 12 minutes. Pour out most of the water until the level is half way up potatoes. Add kale, reduce the heat to medium-low, cover and simmer until potatoes are very soft. Empty entire pot into a colander and drain well. Add back to the pot and add pepper, butter and green onion tops. Use a fork or potato masher and roughly smash potatoes, leaving a few nice chunks for texture. Adjust seasoning with a little more salt, particularly if you used unsalted butter.

For the salmon: Preheat oven to 225°F (110°C) and a nonstick skillet to medium-high. It is preferable to use a skillet that has an ovensafe handle. Brush a little oil onto flesh side of salmon only, just enough to achieve a lovely caramel colour on the presentation side of the fillet. Season each side of fish with a little salt and pepper and place, flesh side down, into the skillet. You should hear an intense sizzle if the pan is hot enough. Cook for 3 minutes on that side and then gently flip with a spatula onto the skin side. Add butter to the pan and place in the oven for 6 to 8 minutes. Remove salmon from pan and, if desired, remove skin. Some people enjoy eating the crispy skin as well.

Serve with a heaping tablespoonful of green tomato chow alongside a heaping portion of delicious Irish colcannon.

Serves 6

Roast Black Cod on Rock Crab Asian Vegetable Orzo Pasta

Black cod, or sablefish, is a hot new item in the culinary world. Native to British Columbia, the fish is popular for its buttery texture (hence its other name *butterfish*) and versatility. Think of it as halibut with the fat content of salmon. It is a delicate fish that needs to be handled with care during the cooking process. Asian-inspired flavours and the very freshest ingredients make the simple vegetable and pasta dish on the side uncommonly good. This sauce works well as a glaze, marinade or vinaigrette for hot or cold salads.

Fish

2 tbsp (30 mL) peanut oil
4 x 6-oz (180-g) pieces fresh black cod (sablefish)
sea salt
freshly ground black pepper

Pasta

½ cup (125 mL) julienne of snow peas
½ cup (125 mL) julienne of carrot
½ cup (125 mL) julienne of red pepper
½ cup (125 mL) julienne of yellow pepper
½ cup (125 mL) sliced shiitake mushrooms
2 cups (500 mL) chopped bok choy
1 tbsp (15 mL) grated fresh ginger
2 cloves garlic, crushed
4 tbsp (60 mL) peanut oil
1 cup (250 mL) cooked orzo pasta
¾ cup (180 mL) or 1 can cooked rock crab meat
¼ cup (80 mL) Asian Vinaigrette (recipe follows)
¼ cup (80 mL) sliced green onion tops
1 tsp (5 mL) cornstarch
2 tsp (10 mL) water

Garnish

3 tbsp (45 mL) sliced pickled ginger
1 tbsp (15 mL) toasted sesame seeds

Asian vinaigrette

1 tbsp (15 mL) crushed garlic
2 tbsp (15 mL) grated fresh ginger
1 tsp (5 mL) Chinese five-spice
½ cup (125 mL) peanut oil
2 cups (500 mL) light soy sauce
1 cup (250 mL) mirin (sweet cooking wine)
1 cup (250 mL) rice wine vinegar
¼ cup (80 mL) toasted sesame oil
1 tbsp (15 mL) hot chili sauce
3/4 cup (180 mL) honey

For the fish: Preheat a nonstick sauté pan over high heat with peanut oil and sear black cod on both sides for 90 seconds. The fillet has varying thicknesses so be careful to adjust cooking time, depending on the portion size. Season with a little salt and pepper.

For the pasta: Sauté snow peas, carrot, red and yellow peppers, mushrooms, bok choy, ginger and garlic in peanut oil in a very hot pan for 3 minutes. Add orzo pasta, cooked using the instructions on the box. Add crab meat, Asian Vinaigrette and green onion tops and bring to a boil. Immediately add a slurry of cornstarch and water to slightly thicken the sauce.

To serve, place cod on a pile of the hot orzo pasta and garnish with a sprinkle of pickled ginger and toasted sesame seeds.

Serves 4

For the vinaigrette: Sauté garlic, ginger and five-spice powder in 3 tablespoons (245 mL) peanut oil on medium-low heat for 3 minutes. Add to all other ingredients in a mixing bowl and whisk together. Store, refrigerated, for up to 3 months in a sealed container.

Yields 6 cups (1.5 L)

Meat

Meat is usually the star of the show — just imagine Christmas without a turkey or a summer barbecue without a thick-cut steak. Meat eaters are passionate about their protein.

The wonderful thing these days about shopping for chicken, pork, beef, lamb or any other favourite meat is the growing number of small suppliers that are accessible. Not only are farmers showing up at local markets each week, but small butcher shops also seem to be standing strong against the supermarket giants. More and more people today are buying "free-range" and "organically fed" meat in an age when tastes are discerning and additives are feared.

You will see from several of the dishes I present here that I have a particular interest in the art of charcuterie. Sausages, bacon, dry-aged beef and ham, pancetta and smoked meats are delicious additions to our menus that also keep centuries-old traditions alive in villages across our country. These products highlight the multicultural influences within Canadian cuisine — particularly those of European nations — and make an important contribution to many local economies.

It is important to understand the proper use of heat when roasting, frying, grilling and stewing meat. Sometimes flavour is built by searing and caramelizing protein over high heat, and at other times by simmering gently under savoury broths. Every cut has its own set of rules that must be followed to achieve success, so stick to the heat settings in these recipes carefully. And don't forget the importance of seasoning — do not shy away from salt and pepper for any of your favourite meat dishes.

Lamb Wellington with Chanterelles

Beef Wellington, a classic dish often served with pâté de foie gras and mushroom *duxelles*, has a long history. The idea of wrapping lamb in puff pastry is not new either, but accompanied by chanterelle mushrooms it takes on a distinctly seasonal feel. Chanterelles are mostly available in the summer, but many foragers sell late spring crops at markets.

1 lamb loin (10 to 12 oz/300 to 360 g)
salt and pepper to season
1 tbsp (15 mL) olive oil
1 lb (450 g) fresh chanterelle mushrooms, cleaned
1 tbsp (15 mL) butter
1 shallot, minced
1 clove garlic, minced
¼ tsp (1 mL) salt
¼ tsp (1 mL) pepper
1 sheet frozen puff pastry (10 x 12 in (25 x 30 cm)
½ cup (125 mL) country pork pâté
2 egg yolks, beaten
1 tsp (5 mL) rock salt or fleur de sel

Sear seasoned lamb loin in oil in a very hot pan for 1 minute per side. Do not cook the meat through — this step is only to build flavour. Rest meat on a rack until cool to the touch.

Set aside the nicest-looking ½ lb (225 g) of chanterelle mushrooms. They will be sautéed and used as garnish later. The smaller and more "imperfect" mushrooms will be made into a duxelles, a sort of simple mushroom pâté. Process these chanterelles in a food processor until they are finely chopped and look wet. Place in a nonstick pan with butter, shallot, garlic, salt and pepper. Cook for 15 minutes over medium-low heat until the duxelles releases its water and it evaporates. Remove from pan and chill completely in the refrigerator.

Trim puff pastry sheet until it is roughly 10 x 7 in (25 x 18 cm), with the long side closest to you. Leaving a 1-in (2.5-cm) border, spread pork pâté evenly over dough. Spread duxelles directly over pâté. Place seared and chilled lamb loin on the duxelles closest to you. Brush beaten egg yolk around the untreated border of dough and slowly roll away from you. The eggwash will seal the dough. Place the seal underneath the roll to secure it well and brush more eggwash over entire Wellington. Sprinkle with salt and bake in a 450°F (230°C) oven for 5 to 7 minutes, only until crust is golden brown. Do not overcook meat in the middle. Rest for several minutes before slicing into 1 ½-in (4-cm) thick pieces.

Sauté remaining chanterelle mushrooms in a little butter with salt and pepper and serve alongside the Lamb Wellington. The lamb can be served in a single 2-in (5-cm) thick slice or two smaller slices if desired.

Serves 4

Braised Nova Scotia Lamb Shank, Charred Vegetable Rice Pilaf, Tzatziki and Natural Jus

This dish pays homage to the large Lebanese and Greek communities in Halifax and recognizes the huge influence they have had on our food culture. Pairing familiar Mediterranean flavours with the very best Nova Scotia lamb results in a delicious meal. Small lamb producers are raising fantastic lamb in every province of Canada. Take the time to source the local stuff and you will be very pleased with the results.

Lamb···
6 lamb shanks (usually about 12 oz/340 g each)
½ cup (125 mL) canola oil
1 large onion, coarsely chopped
2 stalks celery, coarsely chopped
2 medium-sized carrots, coarsely chopped
2 cloves whole garlic
2 cups (500 m) dry sherry
2 cups (500 mL) medium-bodied red wine (Merlot or Shiraz)
4 cups (1 L) beef stock (lamb is preferable but is often not available)
6 sprigs fresh oregano
4 sprigs fresh mint
6 bay leaves
salt and pepper, to taste

Rice pilaf···
1 red onion
1 green zucchini
1 small eggplant
1 red pepper
1 yellow pepper
1 cup (250 mL) cherry tomatoes
3 cloves garlic, minced
¼ cup (60 mL) extra-virgin olive oil
1 ½ cups (375 mL) basmati rice
2 tsp (10 mL) freshly ground black pepper
1 tsp (10 mL) salt
3 ½ cups (875 mL) low-sodium chicken broth
1 ½ cups (375 mL) lamb braising liquid, optional
¼ cup (60 mL) chopped fresh oregano
½ cup (125 mL) crumbled feta cheese

Tzatziki···
1 English cucumber, unpeeled but seeded
1 tbsp (15 mL) sea salt
2 cups (500 mL) thick natural Greek yogurt*
1 tbsp (15 mL) white wine vinegar
juice and zest of ½ lemon
1 tbsp (15 mL) extra-virgin olive oil
1 clove garlic, minced (germ in centre removed)
2 tsp (10 mL) chopped mint or dill

¼ tsp (1 mL) freshly ground black pepper
2 drops Tabasco sauce
¼ tsp (1 mL) salt

For the lamb: Pan-roast lamb shanks in canola oil over medium-high heat until golden brown on all sides (about 3 minutes per side). Remove from the pan and place in a braising dish or steep-sided roasting pan. Remove excess oil from the pan and sauté onion, celery, carrots and garlic for 10 minutes, until slightly caramelized. Deglaze the pan with sherry. Add all vegetables, wine, stock and herbs to the braising dish. There should be enough liquid to completely cover the shanks.

Bring dish to the boil, transfer to a 300°F (150°C) oven and braise for 2 ½ to 3 hours. The meat will flake away from the bone easily when tested with a fork. Remove from oven and let shanks set in the braising liquor for 1 hour. Remove shanks to a serving platter, cover with plastic wrap and set in warm place. Strain braising liquor into a saucepan and reduce over medium heat by two-thirds until sauce will coat the back of a wooden spoon. Season sauce with a little salt and pepper *after* the reduction is complete to ensure the sauce is not too salty.

For the rice pilaf: Cut onion, zucchini and eggplant into ½-in (1-cm) thick slices. The peppers can be left whole until they are grilled. Using a barbecue grill or a stovetop grill pan, char onion, zucchini, eggplant and peppers until well caramelized. The peppers can be left on much longer, until the skin is well blackened, and then it will peel off easily under a tap or after a short rest in a covered bowl. Once all the vegetables are charred, roughly dice them and set aside. It is not necessary to grill the cherry tomatoes but they can be slightly charred if desired.

In a steep-sided braising pan or saucepan, sweat garlic in olive oil for 3 minutes over medium heat. Add rice, pepper and salt and stir well to coat rice with the oil. Add the stocks. If you do not have lamb stock use chicken or beef broth. Add vegetables and cherry tomatoes to rice and cover. Bring to a boil and immediately place in a 300°F (150°C) oven for 15 to 20 minutes, or until all the liquid is absorbed into the rice. Remove from the oven and fluff the rice with a fork. Stir in fresh oregano and feta cheese just prior to serving.

For the tzatziki: Grate seeded cucumber into a bowl and toss with the tablespoon of sea salt. Place in a sieve over an empty bowl in the refrigerator for 2 hours. Remove from the refrigerator and squeeze out as much of the water as possible. Place cucumber in a clean bowl and mix thoroughly with all remaining ingredients *except* the last ¼ teaspoon of salt. Taste before adding any further salt, as it may not be necessary.

Serve each lamb shank on a heaping mound of rice. Top with the aromatic jus and garnish with tzatziki and fresh herbs such as oregano, chives, or basil.

* This recipe requires a proper Greek yogurt, which is much thicker than many Canadian brands. A looser-style yogurt can be used but it should be sieved overnight to extract some of the water. Simply place yogurt in a sieve, rest it over an empty bowl and refrigerate. Gravity alone will extract water and the yogurt will be much thicker by morning.

Serves 6

Grilled Lamb Chops "Gremolata" with Parsley Root Purée and Blueberry Jus

This may sound like a complicated appetizer, but it is actually very easy to make and impressive in presentation. Although most of the ingredients here are available year-round, parsley root is a little hard to find except in the late summer months. You can use celery root, potato or even turnip instead and the results will be very enjoyable. Lamb chops should always be cut very thick, so that the tender meat will not overcook before a good, flavourful crust develops during the sear.

Chops
6 lamb chops, about 1-in (2.5-cm) thick (3 oz or 90 g each)
1 tsp (5 mL) dried mint
½ tsp (3 mL) freshly ground black pepper
3 tbsp (45 mL) canola oil
½ tsp (3 mL) fleur de sel

Purée
1 lb (450 g) parsley root, peeled and coarsely chopped
¼ cup (60 mL) extra-virgin olive oil
½ tsp (3 mL) sea salt
¼ tsp (1 mL) pepper
2 tbsp (30 mL) chopped Italian parsley

Gremolata
1 garlic clove, finely chopped
3 tbsp (45 mL) Italian parsley, finely chopped
1 tsp (5 mL) grated lemon zest

Blueberry jus
½ shallot, minced
½ tsp (2 mL) freshly grated ginger
¼ cup (60 mL) port wine
1 cup (250 mL) wild blueberries (lowbush variety)
1 tbsp (15 mL) Demi Glace, optional (see recipe in "Basics" chapter)
⅛ tsp (0.5 mL) salt

For the lamb chops: Heat a nonstick skillet to medium-high. Rub the outside of each lamb chop with mint and pepper and sear in oil on each side until deep brown in colour. Place the skillet in a 250°F (120°C) oven for 5 minutes. Remove chops from oven and rest for 5 minutes on a rack. Sprinkle with a little fleur de sel before serving.

For the parsley root purée: Steam parsley root in a double boiler until fork-tender. Place cooked root in a food processor and blend on high. Slowly add olive oil and season with salt and pepper. Remove from the food processor and fold in chopped parsley.

For the gremolata: Combine all the ingredients in a bowl and mix well.

For the blueberry jus: Combine shallot, ginger and wine in a small saucepan and reduce liquid by one-half. Add the blueberries and Demi Glace and simmer for 30 minutes. Season with salt. If you do not use Demi Glace the sauce may be a little thin, so a small amount of cornstarch and water may be necessary.

To serve, make a small pile of purée on each plate and place a chop on top. Sprinkle with a teaspoon of gremolata and drizzle warm blueberry sauce over and around the plate.

Serves 6

Bacon-wrapped Berkshire Pork Chop, Polenta, Succotash and Barbecue Anise Jus

Bacon-wrapping foods in my restaurant just seems so Canadian. We do it for two reasons: for flavour and for moisture retention in the meat. This process, known as barding, is a very old one and is especially useful when trying to keep leaner cuts of meat tender and moist. Pork loin is a great cut for this method of cooking, even though Berkshire and heritage pork products are generally better for roasting and keep moist longer.

Pork loin·······································
1 5-lb (2.3-kg) Berkshire pork loin, bone in
1 tsp (5 mL) pepper
1 lb (450 g) thinly sliced streaky bacon

Succotash·······································
4 cobs of corn
½ cup (125 mL) diced red pepper
½ cup (125 mL) diced green pepper
½ cup (125 mL) diced red onion
1 clove garlic, finely chopped
¾ cup (180 mL) blanched lima beans or tinned green flageolet beans
¾ cup (180 mL) halved cherry tomatoes
¼ cup (60 mL) butter
1 tsp (5 mL) salt
½ tsp (3 mL) freshly ground black pepper
3 tbsp (45 mL) chopped fresh sage
3 tbsp (45 mL) chopped fresh parsley

Polenta·······································
1 cup (250 mL) minced onion
1 clove garlic, minced
½ cup (125 mL) minced celery
3 bay leaves
3 sprigs fresh sage
4 to 6 cleaned cobs (reserved from succotash recipe)
1 cup (250 mL) fresh kernel corn, optional
4 cups (1 L) chicken broth
2 cups (500 mL) milk
1 tsp (5 mL) sea salt
1 tsp (5 mL) pepper
1 cup (250 mL) yellow cornmeal
¾ cup (280 mL) grated aged white cheddar cheese, Parmesan, or smoked Gouda
¼ cup (60 mL) salted butter

Barbecue anise jus·······························
1 shallot, coarsely chopped
½ cup (125 mL) chopped fresh anise (fennel bulb)
1 clove garlic, coarsely chopped
1 pod star anise
1 cup (250 mL) red wine
⅔ cup (165 mL) ketchup
1 tbsp (15 mL) Dijon mustard
2 tbsp (30 mL) tarragon vinegar
3 tbsp (45 mL) brown sugar
2 tbsp (30 mL) Worcestershire sauce

Ask your butcher to prepare the loin as a "French rack," in which the bones are cleaned and exposed on top of the roast. You can do this easily yourself by cutting between each bone and scraping all the sinew and fat from each rib.

For the pork loin: Season loin with pepper. Allow bacon to come to room temperature, as it will then stretch more easily. Begin wrapping the first slice of bacon on one end of the loin. Start the next slice overlapping the end of the previous one. Obviously the bacon will clump and be thicker in between the bones but this will render out and help to baste the meat while it is in the oven. Secure the final piece by tucking it under the end or by using a toothpick.

Roast loin, with bones standing upright, at 250°F (120°C) for 55 to 70 minutes depending on the type of oven. Use a meat thermometer and remove from the oven when the internal temperature is 130°F (55°C). Rest meat for 30 minutes before cutting.

For the succotash: Carefully remove kernels of corn from the cobs and reserve the cobs for the polenta. Sauté corn, peppers, onion, garlic, beans and tomatoes in butter until corn begins to "snap." Season with salt and pepper and stir in fresh herbs at the very end.

For the polenta: Combine onion, garlic, celery, bay leaves, sage, cobs, kernel corn, chicken broth, milk, salt and pepper together in a thick-bottomed stockpot. Bring to a boil and simmer for 1 hour. Remove the fresh herbs and cobs and begin adding cornmeal in a slow steady stream, whisking continuously. The mixture will begin to thicken. When all the cornmeal is added simmer over very low heat, covered, for 1 hour. Stir frequently to prevent sticking. When the polenta is creamy and not granular in the mouth, stir in cheese and butter and rest for 5 minutes before serving.

For the barbecue anise jus: Combine all ingredients in a small saucepan and simmer for 1 hour. Reduce liquid by one-third and purée in a blender. Strain sauce through a sieve or fine-meshed chinois. Adjust seasoning with a pinch of salt or a couple of drops of Tabasco sauce if desired.

To serve the dish, choose a large pasta bowl or soup plate. Spoon about ½ cup (125 mL) of polenta into the centre of the bowl. Add some succotash on top, then place the rested pork on top of the succotash. Ladle or "nappe" some of the barbecue jus over the pork and serve immediately.

Serves 8 to 10

Lamb Back Ribs with Molasses and Sweet Onion Barbecue Sauce

From time to time short-term volunteer cooks come to Chives to learn how we cook. One day I needed a recipe for a sticky molasses barbecue sauce to accompany some lamb back ribs that I had found at the farmers' market. Lisa, my "commis for a day," came up with the recipe that follows.

Lamb ribs

4 sides of lamb back ribs (about 8 oz/225 g each)
1 small onion, coarsely chopped
1 small carrot, coarsely chopped
½ stalk celery, coarsely chopped
2 cloves garlic, coarsely chopped
1 pod star anise
2 cups (500 mL) sherry or red wine
2 cups (500 mL) lamb broth (if available) or beef Demi Glace (see recipe in "Basics" chapter)
1 cup (250 mL) Molasses and Sweet Onion Barbecue Sauce (recipe follows)

Molasses and sweet onion barbecue sauce

3 cups (750 mL) sliced Vidalia onions
3 cloves garlic, left whole
2 tbsp (30 mL) butter
2 tbsp (30 mL) extra-virgin olive oil
1 cup (250 mL) molasses
⅓ cup (80 mL) apple cider vinegar
¼ cup (60 mL) tomato paste
1 tsp (5 mL) liquid smoke
¼ tsp (1 ml) ground cloves
1 tbsp (15 mL) mustard powder
1 cup (250 mL) crushed pineapple
¼ cup (60 mL) sake (rice wine)
1 tsp (5 mL) Tabasco or other hot sauce
1 tsp (5 mL) sea salt

For the lamb ribs: Using a butter knife, remove the thin membrane from bone side of ribs. It should peel away from the bone easily in one steady pull. If possible, preheat barbecue grill to high and sear ribs for 2 minutes on each side. (You can also sear in a skillet using a couple of tablespoons of canola or olive oil.)

Combine all ingredients except barbecue sauce in a casserole dish or small braising pan and bring to a boil. Immediately lower the heat to a simmer *or* place the ribs in a 250°F (120°C) oven and braise, covered, for 1 hour. The meat on the bones should flake off easily with fork. Cool ribs completely in braising liquid. Remove from liquid and pat dry with a paper towel. The braising liquid can be reserved for use in a soup or frozen for the next time you prepare the recipe.

Reheat ribs on a barbecue grill over medium heat. Brush liberally with barbecue sauce once ribs have developed some colour.

Serves 6 to 8

For the molasses sauce: In a large saucepan, slowly caramelize sliced onions and garlic over medium heat in butter and olive oil for 30 to 45 minutes. The onions should be deep brown in colour and look "sticky." Add all remaining ingredients and simmer for 20 minutes. Purée sauce in a blender and refrigerate in a sealed jar.

Yields 3 ½ cups (875 mL)

Darren's Coq au Vin

Darren Lewis, my business partner and Chef de Cuisine at Chives, has made this several times over the years. Free-range chicken leg and thigh quarters and double-smoked German bacon are ideal for this recipe, and boiled baby potatoes and fresh green beans or *haricots vert* make an excellent accompaniment to a classic *coq au vin*.

2 tsp (10 mL) tomato paste
1 bottle (750 mL) good dry red wine
1 tsp (5 mL) sea salt
½ tsp (3 mL) freshly ground black pepper
2 bay leaves
4 sprigs fresh thyme
6 free-range chicken leg and thigh quarters, skin on
2 tbsp (30 mL) olive oil
½ lb (225 g) double-smoked bacon, chopped
2 tsp (10 mL) butter
20 pearl onions, blanched and peeled
1 head of garlic, peeled, whole cloves
½ lb (225 g) halved button mushrooms
1 Portobello mushroom, stem and gills removed
2 tbsp (30 mL) flour
¼ cup (60 mL) brandy

In a large bowl, combine tomato paste, wine, salt, pepper, bay leaves and thyme and marinate chicken legs for at least 12 hours in the refrigerator. Remove chicken from marinade and pat dry with a paper towel. Reserve marinade for the sauce. Sear chicken in olive oil until both sides are browned. Remove from the pan and rest on a side plate for a few minutes.

Remove any fat from the pan and sauté bacon over medium heat until fat is rendered out and bacon is browned. The bacon fat can be discarded if desired, but keeping it for the base sauce adds tremendous flavour. Set aside bacon with the chicken.

Add butter to the sauté pan and cook onions, garlic and mushrooms for about 10 minutes. When mushroom and onion mixture has some colour add flour and mix well to form a roux with the fat in the pan. *Carefully* deglaze the pan with brandy (it will ignite easily over an open flame) and return reserved marinade to the pan. Stir well to form a slightly thickened sauce. Return chicken and bacon to the pan and simmer, covered, for 30 minutes.

Serves 4 to 6

Braised Beef Short Ribs, White Cheddar Gnocchi, Tarragon Carrots and Fried Shallots

Braising beef ribs is a wonderful way to enjoy beef at a reasonable price. If properly prepared they are much more flavourful than regular stewing beef, primarily because of the bone and higher fat content. I buy my beef directly from a local family-run farm. Gnocchi is one of the world's most perfect foods. Follow the recipe for Four Cheese Gnocchi (see recipe in "Pasta, Risotto and Side Dishes" chapter), but substitute a good-quality aged Canadian cheddar, and the result will be perfect.

Ribs
4 lb (2 kg) beef short ribs, bone-in
3 tbsp (45 mL) canola oil
1 small onion, chopped
½ cup (125 mL) Roasted Garlic Purée (see recipe in "Basics")
2 cups (500 mL) red wine
3 tbsp (45 mL) Dijon mustard
3 sprigs fresh rosemary
2 cups (500 mL) beef broth
2 cups (500 mL) Demi Glace (see recipe in "Basics")

Carrots
3 medium-sized carrots, peeled
1 cup (250 mL) water
¼ tsp (1 mL) sea salt
3 tbsp (45 mL) salted butter
½ tsp (3 mL) brown sugar
½ tsp (3 mL) tarragon vinegar
¼ tsp (1 mL) freshly ground black pepper
1 tbsp (15 mL) coarsely chopped fresh tarragon

Shallots
4 large shallots, sliced thinly
½ cup (125 mL) buttermilk
2 cups (500 mL) canola oil
½ cup (125 mL) cornstarch
⅛ tsp (1/2 mL) sea salt

For the ribs: Sear short ribs in a skillet in canola oil until dark and golden brown. Place in a casserole dish in a single layer, meat side down, bone side up. Remove all but 2 tablespoons of beef fat from the skillet and sauté onion until slightly browned. Add Roasted Garlic Purée and deglaze the pan with red wine. Bring to a boil and pour over short ribs in the casserole dish. Add mustard, rosemary, beef broth and Demi Glace and cover the dish with aluminum foil or an appropriate lid. Braise in a 300°F (150°C) oven for 2 hours, or until meat is falling off the bone. Strain off braising liquid and bring it to a boil in a separate saucepan. Reduce by one-half or until slightly thickened. Pour reduced sauce back over ribs and serve.

For the tarragon carrots: Cut carrots lengthwise and then on an exaggerated bias to ¼-in (7-mm) thickness. Do not slice them too thinly or they will become overcooked. In a saucepan, bring carrots, water and salt to a boil. It is important to use a wide-bottomed saucepan and keep carrots in a 1- to 1 ½-in (2.5- to 4-cm) thick layer on the bottom. When all but ¼ cup (60 mL) of water remains in the pan, add butter, brown sugar, vinegar and black pepper. Continue cooking until the pan goes dry, watching it carefully so that it doesn't burn. The butter and sugar will produce a nice glaze on the carrots. Toss with fresh tarragon and serve.

For the fried shallots: Separate shallot rings carefully with your fingers. Soak for 3 hours in buttermilk. Preheat canola oil in a steep-sided pot to 325°F (165°C) using a deep fry thermometer. Remove shallots from milk and dust with cornstarch. Fry until golden-brown and crisp. Season with sea salt and serve.

To serve the dish, start with a large spoonful of creamy gnocchi. Place some of the carrots on top in a small pile. Place the ribs on top and garnish with the crispy shallots.

Serves 6

Grain-fed Veal Tenderloin, Caramelized Digby Scallops and Carrot "Hollandaise"

This recipe is an example of how good technique and good ingredients combine to make a great meal. The carrot hollandaise is a little "new age," but the recipe evolved from a desire to capture the intensity of perfectly sweet carrots in a sauce. You will need a juicer to do it right, but if you purée the carrot and strain it well you will come very close to the same result. If you prefer, you can substitute beef tenderloin or even rack of lamb in place of veal.

Veal
2 lb (900 g) cleaned veal tenderloin
2 tsp (10 mL) sea salt
2 tsp (10 mL) freshly ground black pepper
½ cup (125 mL) light olive oil or canola oil
18 sea scallops (10-20 count per lb)

Carrot "hollandaise"
1 lb (450 g) carrots, juiced
1 shallot, minced
½ tsp (3 mL) white wine vinegar
1 bay leaf
1 tbsp (15 mL) coarsely chopped ginger
1 egg yolk
½ cup (60 mL) cold salted butter, cubed
⅛ tsp (1/2 mL) freshly ground black pepper

For the veal: Using butcher's twine tie veal with 1-in (2.5-cm) gaps between each knot. This will keep the tenderloin cylindrical in shape as it roasts. Season veal with salt and pepper and sear in a few teaspoons of oil in a large skillet. Remove from oil and place on an elevated roasting rack in a 180°F (80°C) oven for 1 hour. When an internal thermometer reads 130°F (55°C), remove from the oven and rest in a warm place for 30 minutes before carving.

Heat a nonstick pan over high heat and add 3 tbsp (45 mL) of oil. Sear scallops on the largest flat side for 90 seconds, keeping the heat very high. This will become your presentation side on the plate. Flip each scallop to the second side and immediately remove pan from the burner. Allow scallops to rest in the hot pan for 2 minutes. Season with a little sea salt (fleur de sel) and pepper.

For the carrot "hollandaise": Boil carrot juice, shallot, vinegar, bay leaf and ginger in a saucepan and reduce until ½ cup (125 mL) of liquid remains. Strain the reduction into a clean bowl. In a second bowl, beat egg yolk and temper it by adding carrot reduction in small amounts. Whisk in cubes of cold butter. It may become necessary to put the bowl over a pot of simmering water once or twice to melt the butter. Season sauce with a little pepper and serve immediately.

To serve the dish, slice the veal into 1-in (2.5-cm) thick slices allowing 2 slices per person. Place scallops around and even on top of the veal and drizzle carrot hollandaise over the plate. The dish can be served with baby or creamy potatoes, asparagus, or another market-fresh vegetable.

Serves 6

Roast Chicken with Root Vegetables (Poulet Roti)

Julia Child often commented that a cook's ability is determined by how perfectly he or she roasts a chicken. She was a believer in trussing the bird to preserve its juices, as well as for presentation. Very few people are prepared to make the effort to truss their chicken, so this recipe focuses more on the timing and basting of the bird during the roast. Locally produced free-range chickens are generally available at specialty grocery stores or your local farmers' market. For simplicity, the root vegetables accompanying this dish can be placed in the same pan as the chicken, but the higher moisture content may prevent the chicken from developing a crispy skin. I suggest cooking them separately to achieve the ultimate roast.

Roast chicken

1 x 3 ½ to 4 lb (1 ½ to 2 kg) free-range roasting chicken
¼ cup (60 mL) softened butter
2 tsp (10 mL) kosher or coarse sea salt
1 tsp (5 mL) freshly ground black pepper
2 sprigs fresh thyme
2 sprigs fresh rosemary
several leaves fresh sage
bunch of chervil, optional

Roasted vegetables

3 medium-sized potatoes, peeled
1 small celery root, peeled and diced into 1-in (2.5-cm) cubes
1 lb (450 g) baby carrots, with green tops on if available
½ medium-sized turnip, diced
1 sweet potato, diced
3 tbsp (45 mL) extra-virgin olive oil
1 tsp (5 mL) dried sage
3 tbsp (45 mL) melted butter
1 tsp (5 mL) sea salt
1 tsp (5 mL) ground black pepper

For the roast chicken: Rinse chicken well under cold water and pat dry with a clean towel. Rub entire bird, including internal cavity, with soft butter. Sprinkle with salt and pepper and fill cavity with fresh herbs. The herbs can also be chopped, added to the butter and rubbed over the skin if desired.

Preheat oven to 425°F (220°C). It is essential to roast your chicken on an elevated roasting rack. This allows the pan drippings to fall away from the skin and also allows hot air to flow around the body. Roast, breast side up, for 15 minutes. Lower the heat to 350°F (180°C) and continue roasting for a further 15 minutes. At this point carefully flip the chicken over so the backbone is facing the top of the oven. Roast for another 15 minutes, basting as often as possible. When chicken has been in the oven for a total of 45 minutes, flip it back over so the breast side is facing up again. Continue roasting for 30 to 45 minutes or until an internal thermometer reads 170 to 175°F (75 to 80°C). A bird of 4 pounds should take about 75 to 90 minutes total.

For the roasted root vegetables: Cook potatoes in boiling water until tender. (Cooking the potatoes first allows them to be soft inside but crisp and golden outside.) Cut potatoes into wedges and place in a bowl with all other ingredients. Gently toss together and place on a nonstick roasting tray. Roast at 350°F (180°C) for 45 minutes, or until golden brown.

Serves 4 to 6

Ris de Veau with Sweet-and-Sour King Apples and Sweet Potato Frites

Ris de veau, or sweetbreads, consist of the thymus gland of a young calf. Offal meats are not overly common in our culture, but sweetbreads are certainly found on many restaurant menus. They have a wonderful creamy texture, mild flavour and in no way should they be avoided. The key is to prepare them properly by soaking, blanching and peeling before the final fry-up. King apples are locally grown in Nova Scotia and are a heritage apple. Choose your own favorite apple for this recipe if you cannot find the delicious King.

Sweetbreads
1 lb (450 g) veal sweetbreads
2 cups (500 mL) milk
2 tbsp (30 mL) salt
1 gallon (4 L) cold water
½ cup (125 mL) unbleached white flour
1 tsp (5 mL) paprika
1 tsp (5 mL) salt
1 tsp (5 mL) pepper
½ tsp (3 mL) cumin
⅛ tsp (1/2 mL) cayenne pepper
¼ cup (60 mL) clarified butter

Apples
2 large King apples
4 tbsp (60 mL) butter
1 tsp (5 mL) freshly grated ginger
2 tbsp (10 mL) cognac or apple brandy such as Calvados
2 tbsp (30 mL) brown sugar
2 tbsp (30 mL) apple cider vinegar
⅛ tsp salt
⅛ tsp Tabasco sauce

Frites
1 large sweet potato, peeled
4 cups (1 L) canola oil
1 tsp sea salt

For the sweetbreads: Soak sweetbreads in milk overnight or for a minimum of 4 hours. Discard milk and in a pot, cover sweetbreads with salt and cold water. Bring water to a boil and immediately remove from the heat and allow sweetbreads to cool in the water. Remove and peel off outer membrane and any remaining fat. Pat dry with paper towels and cut into bite-sized pieces if necessary. In a small bowl, combine flour, all spices and seasoning. Toss sweetbreads in flour and fry in clarified butter until golden on all sides.

For the sweet-and-sour King apples: Slice apples through the equator into ⅛-in (2-mm) thick rounds. Use an apple corer to remove seeds in the middle of each slice. Heat a large nonstick frying pan to medium and sauté apples in butter and ginger for 3 minutes. Deglaze the pan with cognac and carefully flambé using a match or the flame of a gas grill. Add brown sugar, vinegar, salt and Tabasco sauce. Remove apples from the pan and reduce the sauce by one-third. Pour sauce over sliced apples and cool.

For the sweet potato frites: You will need a mandoline or Asian "benreemer" vegetable slicer. Julienne sweet potato into very thin, long matchsticks by slicing lengthwise on the fine-toothed blade of the mandoline. Preheat oil in a steep-sided pot to 325°F (165°C). Fry potato matchsticks in small batches until crisp. Place onto a tray lined with paper towels and gently pull apart the strands of sweet potato while they are still hot. Season with salt. In a few moments the frites will become very crispy as they cool.

Serves 6

Free-range Chicken Pub Pie

Perhaps the ultimate comfort food, chicken pot pie is a classic recipe for cold winter nights. That doesn't mean it can't be enjoyed all year round. Resembling a *pâté en croûte*, the rich meat inside is bound in a small amount of sauce, and any vegetables are served on the side, the way that pies are made and served in Britain.

Chicken
1 whole free-range chicken
1 medium onion, coarsely chopped
1 stalk celery, coarsely chopped
1 carrot, coarsely chopped
2 bay leaves
4 sprigs fresh thyme or sage
2 cups (500 mL) unsalted chicken broth
water to cover

Filling
1 small onion, minced
1 stalk celery, minced
1 clove garlic, minced
¼ cup (60 mL) butter
½ tsp (3 mL) dried summer savory
¼ cup (60 mL) flour
¼ cup (60 mL) white wine or sherry
1 ½ cups (375 mL) reserved chicken broth reduction
1 tsp (5 mL) salt
1 tsp (5 mL) freshly ground black pepper
2 tbsp (30 mL) chopped fresh sage
2 tbsp (30 mL) chopped fresh Italian parsley

Pie assembly
1 lb (450 g) Flaky Pie Dough (see recipe in "Basics")
chilled chicken pie filling
1 egg, beaten
1 tsp (5 mL) rock salt or fleur de sel

For the chicken: Combine all ingredients in a stockpot, using enough cold water to cover the bird. Bring to a boil, reduce the heat, and simmer, covered, for 2 hours. Remove from the heat and chill the bird completely *while still in the broth*. This allows the meat to hydrate completely as it cools. When stock is cold, remove chilled fat from the top. Remove chicken and discard all exterior fat and skin. Pick meat completely off the carcass and shred by hand into small pieces. Strain stock and discard vegetables and herbs. Place stock on the heat and reduce to 1 ½ cups (375 mL). Cool reduction completely.

For the filling: Sauté onion, celery and garlic in butter until onions begin to turn slightly brown, about 15 minutes. Add summer savory and flour to form a roux. Stir in white wine or sherry, then add cold chicken broth. Season with salt and pepper. Use a whisk and stir to make very smooth. The mixture should be very thick in consistency, like wallpaper paste. Stir in fresh herbs and add sauce to the picked chicken meat. Adjust seasoning if desired. Refrigerate for 30 minutes before assembling the pie.

For pie assembly: Cut pastry in half and roll each piece into 2 sheets, approximately ¼-in (5-mm) thick. Line a nonstick 9- to 10-in (23- to 25-cm) tart pan with the first layer of pastry. Smaller individual tart pans can also be used, as pictured here. Fill with chicken mixture until it heaps in the middle. Cover with the second piece of pastry and trim the edges. Cut 3 small holes in the top of the pastry to allow steam to escape during baking. Brush with beaten egg and sprinkle with rock salt before baking. Bake for 35 minutes at 350°F (180°C) or until crust is deep brown in colour.

Slice the tart in wedges, as you would a dessert pie, and serve immediately with your favourite vegetables.

Serves 6 to 8

Tourtière Pie

The history of this dish is a long one, and every Christmas Eve thousands of Acadian families enjoy meat pie. Served with crunchy coleslaw, cranberries or a traditional Québécois fruit relish, it is pure heaven. I have tasted this dish all over the Maritimes and Quebec and my personal preference is for a Montreal-area style that includes more spices than the Acadian recipes of New Brunswick.

1 small onion, minced
½ tsp (3 mL) ground clove
½ tsp (3 mL) ground allspice
1 tsp (5 mL) cinnamon
1 tsp (5 mL) summer savory
1 (5 mL) salt
1 tsp (5 mL) pepper
2 tbsp (30 mL) rendered pork or bacon fat
1 lb (450 g) ground beef
1 lb (450 g) ground pork
½ cup (125 mL) beef stock
1 medium-sized waxy potato, unpeeled and grated
1 lb (450 g) Flaky Pie Dough (recipe in "Basics" chapter)
1 egg yolk, beaten
1 tsp (5 mL) rock salt

In a medium-sized, steep-sided pot, sauté onion, spices and seasoning in pork fat until translucent. Add ground beef and pork, stock and grated potato. Stir well to combine as you heat the mixture. Cook for 15 minutes over medium heat, until meat looks fully cooked. Allow filling to cool in the pot while you roll out pie dough into two 12-in (30-cm) rounds. When filling is cool to the touch, add to bottom pie shell, mounding it in the centre of the pie. Cover with a second piece of pie dough and trim the edges with a knife. Using a pastry tip or apple corer make a ½-in (12-mm) vent hole in the centre of top crust. Brush with beaten egg yolk and sprinkle with rock salt. Bake in a preheated 350°F (180°C) oven for 45 minutes or until crust is deep brown in colour.

Serves 6

Ham, Mozzarella and Caramelized Onion-stuffed Chicken with Sweet Potato "Risotto" and Pine Nuts

Chicken dishes are often the "conservative" option on restaurant menus and can be a little bland. This, however, is a very flavourful recipe that can be served with simple mashed potatoes, pasta or the sweet potato dish suggested here.

5 cups (1.25 L) sliced onion
4 cloves garlic, sliced
3 shallots, sliced
2 tbsp (30 mL) olive oil
¼ cup (60 mL) butter
1 tsp (5 mL) salt
1 tsp (5 mL) pepper
¼ cup (60 mL) sherry
½ cup (125 mL) finely chopped Westphalian ham
2 cups (500 mL) diced fresh mozzarella or bocconcini cheese
¼ cup (60 mL) grated Parmesan cheese
¼ cup (60 mL) fine breadcrumbs
3 tbsp (45 mL) chopped chives
8 x 7-oz (200-g) chicken breasts (bone in, skin on)
Sweet Potato "Risotto" (see recipe in "Vegetarian Dishes")

In a wide-bottomed pot, combine onions, garlic, shallots, oil, butter, salt and pepper and cook for 90 minutes to caramelize onions. Start the onions over high heat and then turn it down to *very low*, stirring frequently to prevent sticking. When onions are dark and sticky, add sherry and deglaze the pan. Remove onions and allow them to cool in a mixing bowl.

Add ham, cheeses, breadcrumbs and chives and mix thoroughly. Place stuffing in a piping bag with a wide-mouthed round pastry tip.

To prepare chicken breasts, insert the blade of a paring knife into the thickest part, near the bone end. Hold breast flat against the work surface as you insert the blade, and with a sweeping motion create a cavity for the stuffing. Fill each breast with as much stuffing as possible. Close the cavity with a toothpick and roast at 425°F (215°C) for 12 minutes. Rest chicken for 10 minutes and then slice on the bias through the centre of the breast, exposing the soft filling.

Serve stuffed chicken breasts on a bed of Sweet Potato "Risotto."

Serves 8

Ginger and Sesame-glazed Duck on Sticky Rice with Pak Choi

Duck is one of those dishes that home cooks find intimidating. I believe this is because of the fat content of the skin and not knowing how to properly prepare it. The end result is often a greasy, unpleasant meal. Scoring the duck fat with a knife will allow it to flow out more easily. And in order to render the fat from the skin you have to lower the heat and allow it to melt. Good duck breast should never be cooked beyond medium rare or medium.

One of the best kitchen gadgets I have ever purchased is a rice cooker. Entry-level models are inexpensive and they never overcook the rice. Just follow the instructions on the box for perfect rice every time.

Duck
6 duck breasts (8 oz or 225 g each)
2 tbsp (30 mL) honey
2 tbsp (30 mL) soy sauce
2 tbsp (30 mL) teriyaki sauce
1 tbsp (15 mL) grated fresh ginger
1 tsp (5 mL) toasted sesame oil
1 tsp (5 mL) rice wine vinegar
¼ tsp (1 mL) Tabasco or Asian hot sauce
1 tbsp (15 mL) toasted sesame seeds

Rice
1 x 2-in (5-cm) piece fresh ginger, cut in half
1 stalk lemon grass, cut in half
2 bay leaves
2 cups (500 mL) Asian short-grained rice or sushi rice (such as Rose brand)

Pak choi
6 small pak choi, cut in half
2 tbsp (30 mL) butter
2 tbsp (30 mL) water
½ tsp (3 mL) salt
freshly ground pepper
2 tbsp (30 mL) julienned pickled ginger

For the duck: Using a sharp knife, score each duck breast by cutting ⅛ in (3 mm) into the fat — but do not cut all the way into the meat. Cut in one direction, then the other, making a hatched pattern. In a nonstick skillet, place each breast fat side down, without using any additional oil. Over medium heat at first, render the fat from the breast for 4 minutes. Lower the heat and continue cooking for 5 to 8 additional minutes. Check the skin from time to time and see how the dark golden-brown colour is developing. The amount of oil in the pan will increase slowly during this period. When the skin is brown and crispy to the touch, remove each breast and set aside for a few moments.

Pour out the excess fat from the skillet, but leave about 2 tablespoons. Increase the heat and add duck to the pan again, this time with the flesh side down. Sear for 1 minute, remove the breasts again and set aside. This time remove all the remaining fat and then add honey, soy sauce, teriyaki sauce, ginger, sesame oil, vinegar and hot sauce. Bring to a fast boil and immediately add breasts back to the pan. Coat them in the glaze and place the pan in 350°F (180°C) oven for 6 minutes. Remove breasts from the hot pan and allow to rest (if left in the pan the residual heat will overcook the meat). Slice thinly and drizzle a little of the glaze over the meat. Sprinkle with toasted sesame seeds just prior to serving.

For the sticky rice: Place ginger, lemongrass and bay leaves in the bottom of the tray of your rice cooker. Cover with rice and prepare as per the rice brand's instructions regarding the water content. Remove the aromatics before serving.

For the pak choi: Place all the ingredients in a microwave-safe dish and cook on high power for 3 minutes. The pak choi should be wilted but still crunchy.

To plate the dish, use a ring mould or coffee cup and fill with rice, pressing firmly. Invert the cup and position the rice slightly to the left of centre on a dinner plate. Slice the duck breast into ⅛-in (3 mm) thick slices and fan next to the rice. Garnish with pak choi, pickled ginger, sesame seeds and fresh herbs (see photograph).

Serves 6

Marinated and Grilled Beef Tenderloin with Fork-smashed Potatoes and Oyster Mushrooms

Nothing gets beef eaters excited like a filet. Filet is tender but not the most flavourful cut, so I spice it up with a killer marinade. The recipe that follows is my personal favourite, as it goes well with a classic potato side dish.

Marinade and beef

¼ cup (60 mL) Worcestershire sauce
1 clove garlic, halved
½ tsp (3 mL) Dijon mustard
¼ tsp (1 mL) fresh thyme, optional
¼ tsp (1 mL) fresh rosemary, optional
1 tsp (5 mL) black pepper
⅓ cup (80 mL) canola oil
4 x 8-oz (225-g) filets of beef (highest quality possible, such as AAA or Angus)
1 tsp (5 mL) fleur de sel
8 oz (225 g) oyster mushrooms
2 tbsp (30 mL) butter
pinch of salt and pepper
Fork-smashed Potatoes (recipe follows)

Fork-smashed potatoes

6 medium Yukon gold potatoes
2 tbsp (30 mL) salt
½ cup (125 mL) salted butter
½ cup (125 mL) sour cream
¼ cup (60 mL) sliced chives or green onion tops
1 tsp (5 mL) salt
1 tsp (5 mL) pepper

For the marinade and beef: In a blender, combine Worcestershire sauce, garlic, mustard, thyme, rosemary and pepper. Blend on high until garlic is finely crushed, then add oil slowly through the top of the blender. Store the emulsified marinade in a sealed container for up to 3 weeks in the refrigerator.

Rub each individual filet of beef in a couple of heaping tablespoons of marinade. Refrigerate for at least 24 hours before use. Preheat barbecue grill to high and wipe filets free of any excess marinade before grilling. Cook each filet for 4 minutes on each side. Lower the heat and turn off the front burner completely. Place beef over the unlit burner and allow to slow roast until an internal thermometer reads 120°F (50°C). Rest the filet for 5 minutes before serving.

When ready to serve, cut filet once through the centre (equator) and sprinkle exposed rose-coloured flesh with a little fleur de sel.

Sauté oyster mushrooms in a little butter and season with salt and pepper to taste.

Serve filet of beef with your favourite vegetables, sautéed oyster mushrooms and a heaping spoonful of delicious Fork-smashed Potatoes.

Serves 4

For the potatoes: Cover whole, unpeeled potatoes in water and add 2 tablespoons of salt. Boil until completely cooked and very soft when pierced with a knife. It is best to wait until the skins begin to split before straining the water away. Using a fork, roughly smash potatoes until creamier but still with lots of good-sized chunks. Add butter, sour cream, chives, salt and pepper and stir until butter melts. If you use unsalted butter a little more salt may be required.

Makes 6 healthy portions

Dried Fruit-stuffed Pork Loin with Walnut Blue Cheese Risotto

Warm and soothing, this dish is definitely one for cold winter or fall evenings. However, as it uses dried fruit it is great for any time of year. The fruit filling is sticky but a little tart due to the added vinegar. As suggested here, try it with my Walnut Blue Cheese Risotto (see recipe in "Pasta, Risotto and Side Dishes"). It would go just as well with some creamy potatoes with a little blue cheese stirred in at the end.

Pork

1 whole pork loin (approximately 4 ½ lb/2 kg and 12 in/30 cm in length)
½ cup (125 mL) coarse sea or kosher salt
1 cup (250 mL) brown sugar
3 tbsp (45 mL) dried sage
3 tbsp (45 mL) dried summer savory
2 cloves garlic, minced
8 cups (2 L) cold water

Stuffing

¼ cup (60 mL) seedless raisins
¼ cup (60 mL) chopped prunes
¼ cup (60 mL) chopped dried apricots
¼ cup (60 mL) chopped dried pear
¼ cup (60 mL) chopped dried apple
¼ cup (60 mL) chopped dates
1 apple, peeled and diced
½ cup (125 mL) minced red onion
2 tbsp (30 mL) brown sugar
¼ cup (60 mL) apple cider vinegar
½ cup (125 mL) port wine
¼ tsp (1 mL) powdered cloves
1 tbsp (15 mL) chopped sage
3 tbsp (45 mL) chopped Italian parsley
½ tsp (3 mL) salt
¼ tsp (1 mL) freshly ground black pepper

For the pork loin: Select a long carving knife with a blade no wider than 1 in (2.5 cm). Insert blade through centre of loin, holding blade exactly parallel to the work surface. The object is to create a centre cavity to hold the stuffing. Remove the blade and insert from the other side. The two incisions should meet if you hold the knife steady and straight. Use your fingers and gently stretch the meat out from both sides, widening the cavity.

Mix salt, sugar, herbs, garlic and water in a large bowl and submerge pork loin for 1 hour. Remove and pat dry with a paper towel before stuffing.

For the fruit stuffing: Combine all ingredients in a saucepan and simmer for 1 hour. The apple and onions will melt and slowly form a binding sauce for the chunky fruit. When the mixture looks dry and sticky, remove from the heat and refrigerate.

Place stuffing in a piping bag with the widest tip you can find (wider than the largest piece of fruit in the filling, so it doesn't clog). Insert the tip into one side of pork loin and squeeze out one-half of the filling. Remove and insert from the other side and squeeze out the remainder. Gently roll the loin around with your fingers to distribute the stuffing evenly in the centre. Using two metal skewers pin the ends of the loin together. The ends can also be plugged using some scrap pork meat or a half-strip of bacon.

Preheat oven to 275°F (135°C) and roast for 55 to 65 minutes, or until an internal thermometer reads 150°F (65°C). Allow roasted meat to rest for 30 minutes before slicing into 2-in (5-cm) thick slices.

Serve pork loin on the cut edge to show off the stuffing and to prevent it from oozing out onto the plate.

Serves 6

Vegetarian

Vegetables are still an afterthought for many people, perhaps because we have all experienced soggy, overcooked broccoli and asparagus, or carrots boiled forever and a day for Sunday dinner. But with the growing interest in healthy living, vegetables are finding their place not only in side dishes but also as the main theme of our suppers. Farmers' markets are bustling each week with customers anxious to find the year's first baby spinach greens or fiddleheads. Rice, lentils, chick peas, beans and even tofu are featured on fine dining menus, not because they are trendy or requested by a vegetarian diner, but because they taste delicious.

My favourite vegetable is, without a doubt, the humble onion. It forms the basis of so many recipes that it is hard to even imagine a culinary world without it. An onion can be luscious and sweet or bring tears to your eyes. Its cousin, the chive, has become a symbol in my cooking for its elegance and sophistication, yet it too packs a punch that cannot be ignored.

Now that I grow vegetables myself in the Annapolis Valley for the restaurant, I have learned that nothing we eat should be taken for granted, especially when someone has toiled long and hard to bring it to our tables.

Marinated Globe Artichokes with Olives, Lemon and Oregano

An extremely simple antipasti-style recipe, this dish is especially great if you take the time to prepare fresh globe artichokes from scratch. Serve it on a large platter garnished with fresh tomatoes or blossoming oregano flowers and you will make a picnic table or barbecue supper buffet extraordinary.

12 fresh globe artichokes
2 cloves garlic, minced
juice of 2 lemons
zest of ½ lemon
1 tsp (5 mL) sugar
3 tbsp (45 mL) chopped fresh oregano
1 fresh red chili, minced
½ tsp (3 mL) salt
½ tsp (3 mL) pepper
1 cup (250 mL) oil-cured mixed olives
¼ cup (60 mL) sliced green onion tops
sliced fresh tomatoes for garnish, optional

Peel away outer petals of each artichoke. Using a sharp knife, cut off the top 1 in (2.5 cm) or so. This will expose the inner "choke." Using a peeler remove some of the outer stem as well as the woody bottom part of the vegetable. Steam artichokes for 30 to 40 minutes in 1 in (2.5 cm) of water until they are soft. If any of the petals remain at all woody, remove them. Slice artichoke in half and use a small spoon to scoop out the hairy "choke" in the middle.

In a small bowl mix garlic, lemon juice and zest, sugar, oregano, chili, salt and pepper. Drizzle this dressing over the artichokes and marinate for several hours before serving.

To serve, spread marinated artichokes on a platter. Garnish with olives, green onion tops and sliced fresh tomatoes if desired.

Puttanesca Summer Squash

Although this dish appears in the vegetarian section of this book, it makes a wonderful side dish to grilled or poached fish, such as my Olive Oil-poached Halibut (page 95). Traditionally, puttanesca sauce without the squash is a great sauce for pasta or gnocchi. I like this version because it packs more nutrition into the recipe.

1 green zucchini
1 yellow zucchini
2 cups pattypan squash
1 small red onion, diced
4 cloves garlic, minced
1 tsp (5 mL) chili flakes
¼ cup (60 mL) extra-virgin olive oil
¼ cup (60 mL) red wine or sherry
1 x 8-oz (225-g) tin crushed tomatoes
1 cup (250 mL) grape or cherry tomatoes
½ cup (125 mL) pitted and roughly chopped black olives
¼ cup (60 mL) drained and rinsed capers
½ tsp (3 mL) sea salt
¼ tsp (1 mL) freshly ground black pepper
¼ cup (60 mL) chopped Italian parsley
¼ cup (60 mL) torn basil leaves

Cut each zucchini in half and then into quarters, lengthwise. Angle your knife and remove the piece of pulp in the middle, then cut zucchini into ½-in (1 cm) cubes. The pattypan squash can be left whole if they are very small or cut in half if need be.

Sauté zucchini, squash, onion, garlic and chili flakes in olive oil. Deglaze the pan with wine and add crushed tomatoes, cherry tomatoes, olives and capers. Add salt and pepper and adjust seasoning to your taste. For a spicier sauce a little Tabasco may be added. Simmer for 10 minutes and fold in parsley and basil leaves.

Serves 4 to 6

Fried Green Tomatoes, Braised Lentils, Celery Root Fries, Quince Ginger Chutney and Red Pepper Chili Cream

This entire dish is yet another example of how balance in cooking often elevates the mediocre to the sublime. Here we have crispness with the tomato, richness with the lentils, sweetness and spice with the chutney and creaminess with the red pepper sauce. For vegetarians it is balanced nutritionally, satisfying the need for protein as well.

Fried tomatoes

2 medium-sized green tomatoes
½ cup (125 mL) flour
2 eggs, beaten
½ tsp (3 mL) sea salt
⅛ tsp (0.5 mL) cayenne pepper
1 cup (250 mL) breadcrumbs or cornmeal
½ cup (125 mL) canola oil
½ tsp (3 mL) finishing salt like fleur de sel

Chili cream

2 red peppers
1 dried ancho chili, soaked in water for about an hour
½ tsp (3 mL) chili powder
1 tbsp (5 mL) olive oil
1 tsp (5 mL) Tabasco sauce
¼ cup (60 mL) heavy cream (35% m.f.)
¼ tsp (1 mL) salt

Braised lentils

2 tbsp (30 mL) extra-virgin olive oil
1 shallot, minced
½ stalk celery, minced
1 medium carrot, "brunoise" (cut into ¹⁄₁₆-in: 2-mm dice)
1 clove garlic, minced
1 ¼ cups (310 mL) French Puy or brown lentils
¼ cup (60 mL) wine or sherry (red or white wine is fine)
1 ½ cups (375 mL) vegetable broth
1 tsp (5 mL) Dijon-style mustard
juice of ½ lemon
½ tsp (3 mL) sea salt
½ tsp (3 mL) Tabasco sauce
2 tbsp (30 mL) sliced fresh chives
1 tbsp (15 mL) butter, optional
2 tbsp (30 mL) red pepper chili cream, optional

Celery root fries

1 small celery root, peeled
3 cups (750 mL) canola oil
1 tsp (5 mL) sea salt

Chutney

4 cups (1 L) peeled and diced quince cut into ½-in (1-cm) cubes
½ cup (125 mL) seedless golden raisins
¼ cup (60 mL) minced shallot
1 cup (250 mL) sugar
⅓ cup (80 mL) apple cider vinegar
¼ cup (60 mL) fresh apple cider
⅓ cup (80 mL) grated ginger
1 tbsp (15 mL) dried ginger
⅛ tsp (0.5 mL) ground cloves
1 tsp (5 mL) sea salt

For the fried tomatoes: Slice tomatoes ⅓-in (1-cm) thick and discard end pieces. Dredge slices in flour, then in egg mixture (seasoned with salt and cayenne pepper) and finish in breadcrumbs. Traditional southern recipes often use cornmeal for breading, but I prefer breadcrumbs.

Heat canola oil in a cast-iron pan or electric frying pan to 360 to 375° F (185 to 190°C). These pans keep an even heat. Fry tomatoes until brown and crisp, in a depth of oil that comes about half-way up the sides of the tomatoes. Do not submerge them in oil when frying as they may become greasy. Sprinkle when hot with a little finishing salt and serve immediately.

For the red pepper chili cream: Grill or roast red peppers on your barbecue or over an open propane flame. When the skins are charred and black, place in a covered bowl and allow to sweat for 30 minutes, loosening the charred skins. Remove skin and seeds. Roughly chop with a knife and place in a saucepan with the hydrated ancho chili, chili powder, and olive oil. Sauté for 3 minutes over medium heat. Add Tabasco sauce and cream and bring to a boil. Immediately remove from the heat and purée in a blender while still hot. Be careful to vent the top of the blender properly to prevent the cap from blowing off. Add salt to season the sauce. A little more cream may be necessary, or even water, depending on the initial size of the red peppers. Serve warm.

For the lentils: Heat olive oil in a lidded saucepan and sauté shallot, celery, carrot and garlic for 2 minutes. Add lentils and wine or sherry. Reduce until the pan is dry. Add vegetable broth and reduce the heat to simmer. Cover the pan and simmer for 20 to 30 minutes, until lentils are cooked but still al dente. If a little broth is left in the pot, increase the heat and reduce until all of the broth has been absorbed by the lentils. Stir in mustard, lemon juice, sea salt, Tabasco and chives. Taste and adjust the seasoning if necessary.

A pat of butter at the end will make the lentils creamy and rich. Also, adding 2 tablespoons of red pepper chili cream ties in the flavours of the dish, but it is not required. For a vegan dish do not add the butter.

For the celery root fries: Shred celery root into julienne strips about ⅟₁₆ in (1 mm) thick, using a mandoline or vegetable slicer. This can be done very carefully with a knife, but a mandoline is much more effective. Heat oil to 340°F (170°C). Fry until crisp and golden. Drain on fresh paper towels and season with salt while hot.

For the quince ginger chutney: Prepare by combining all ingredients in a saucepan and cook until all the liquid has evaporated and the chutney is sticky and shimmering. Refrigerate in a covered container until ready for use.

To plate the dish, use a 3-in (7.5-mm) diameter ring mould and fill with the lentils, pressing firmly with the back of a spoon. Place a fried tomato on top of the lentils, garnish with chutney, celery root fries and a drizzle of red pepper sauce around the plate (see photograph).

Serves 6

Grilled Eggplant "Cannelloni" with Olive Oil–poached Field Tomatoes

This "play on words" recipe is a lot of fun and easy to make. The slices of eggplant are grilled and rolled around the ricotta cheese, taking the place of the traditional cylindrical cannelloni pasta. A tiny bit of organization is required with the tomatoes and eggplant, and then the dish comes together into a stunning and elegant presentation.

Eggplant "cannelloni"

1 large eggplant
1 clove garlic, minced
1 tsp (5 mL) dried basil
½ tsp (3 mL) sea salt
½ tsp (3 mL) freshly ground black pepper
¼ cup (60 mL) extra-virgin olive oil

Filling

1 shallot, minced
2 tbsp (30 mL) butter
3 tbsp (45 mL) roasted garlic purée
3 tbsp (45 mL) sherry
2 cups (500 mL) fresh ricotta cheese
2 tbsp (30 mL) chopped chives
2 tbsp (30 mL) chopped fresh basil
1 tsp (5 mL) Tabasco, or your favourite hot chili sauce
1 tsp (5 mL) Worcestershire sauce
¼ cup (60 mL) grated Parmesan cheese

Poached tomatoes

2 cloves garlic
3 sprigs fresh thyme
2 shallots, halved
½ cup (125 mL) sun-dried tomatoes, optional
3 cups (750 mL) extra-virgin olive oil
4 small red field tomatoes
4 small orange or yellow field tomatoes
1 tsp (5 mL) rock salt
1 tsp (5 mL) freshly ground pepper
small herbs of your choice, as garnish

For the eggplant cannelloni: Preheat barbecue or gas grill to high. Cut off 1 in (2.5 cm) from each end of eggplant. Slice from pole to pole (lengthwise) into ½-in (1-cm) thicknesses. Mix all other ingredients in a bowl and brush mixture on both sides of each eggplant slice. Set slices on the grill and cook for 90 seconds. Lift and turn each slice 90 degrees and grill for another 90 seconds. This will create a lovely hatch-marked presentation. Flip eggplant and repeat on the second side.

For the filling: Sauté shallot in butter over medium heat until translucent. Add roasted garlic purée. If you do not have roasted garlic use a single clove of minced fresh garlic. Deglaze the pan with sherry and reduce by one-half, then add to ricotta cheese in a clean bowl. Mix thoroughly with chives, basil, hot sauce, Worcestershire sauce and Parmesan cheese. Refrigerate in a covered bowl until ready for use.

Assemble the "cannelloni" by placing a heaped spoonful of filling in the centre of each slice of grilled eggplant. Roll and place in a pasta bowl with the fold on the bottom. The cannelloni can be served cool, at room temperature or warmed by microwaving it for 30 seconds. Depending on the size of the eggplant slices, this recipe should make 4 to 6 canneloni.

For the olive oil–poached field tomatoes: In a medium-sized saucepan, combine garlic, thyme, shallots, sun-dried tomatoes and olive oil and slowly heat on low until temperature reaches 160°F (70°C). Hold at this temperature for 20 minutes and then reduce the heat until the temperature reaches 110°F (45°C).

Boil a large pot of water, and have a bowl of iced water on hand. Cut a small cross on the bottom of each tomato. Use a knife or tomato corer to remove the stem end. Submerge each tomato in boiling water for 10 seconds and then immediately drop it in the iced water. Use the back of a knife to remove the peel.

Drop each tomato in olive oil and poach for 1 hour, keeping the heat at 110°F (45°C) the entire time.

To serve, place one red and one yellow field tomato next to one large cannelloni in the bowl. Drizzle with some poaching oil, then season tomatoes and cannelloni with rock salt and freshly ground black pepper. Garnish with small herbs like basil or arugula, fresh pea shoots or sliced chives.

Serves 4

Sweet Potato "Risotto" and Pine Nuts

With its beautiful taste and striking visual appeal, this dish would make a lovely vegetarian appetizer. I call it a "risotto" because the method of cooking is as if the balls of sweet potato were actually grains of Italian rice. In this book I have paired it with Ham, Mozzarella and Caramelized Onion Stuffed Chicken (page 122), but it would go equally well with a simple roasted chicken leg, lamb chops or roast pork. To add more protein to this dish, try serving it with an addition of cooked lentils — simply follow the directions and fold in one small tin of green or brown lentils.

1 large onion, minced
1 stalk celery, minced
2 cloves garlic, minced
½ tsp (3 mL) salt
½ tsp (3 mL) freshly ground black pepper
⅛ cup (30 mL) butter
4 large sweet potatoes, peeled
2 to 3 cups (500 mL to 750 mL) very good vegetable stock
¼ cup heavy cream (35% m.f.), optional
¼ cup (60 mL) dry sherry
1 tsp (5 mL) dried summer savory
½ cup (125 mL) grated Parmesan cheese
½ cup (125 mL) toasted pine nuts
2 tbsp (30 mL) chopped fresh sage

In a heavy-bottomed saucepan, slowly cook onion, celery, garlic, salt and pepper in butter for about 30 minutes, until onions caramelize.

While onion mixture is cooking, prepare sweet potatoes. You will need a small melon-ball tool, about ½ in (1 cm) in diameter. Make as many small balls of sweet potato as possible. If you do not have such a tool the recipe can be followed the same way using small dice of sweet potato. The total quantity of potatoes should be about 4 cups (1 L) when completed. The melon baller will leave a fair amount of scrap pieces. Roughly chop these scraps (there will be about 1 cup/250 mL when chopped) and place in a separate small saucepan with ½ cup (125 mL) vegetable stock and heavy cream. Bring to a simmer, and when very soft purée in a blender. Set aside.

When onions are a nutty brown colour, deglaze the pan with sherry and increase the heat. Cook on high until the sherry evaporates. Add summer savory and sweet potato balls and sauté for 3 minutes. Begin adding hot vegetable broth, a ladleful at a time. Cook on medium-high heat until sweet potatoes are tender, but still holding their shape. They may need only 2 cups (500 mL) of broth before they are ready. At this point add about 1 cup (250 mL) of puréed sweet potato sauce made from the scraps. Lower heat to a simmer and cook for another 10 minutes. Add cheese, pine nuts and fresh sage and gently fold together.

Serves 4

Swiss Pan Potato Gratin

I call this dish Swiss Pan Potatoes because during my apprenticeship in Switzerland it was very often our staff supper. It is one of those potato dishes that is a real treat on buffets or as a pot luck supper contribution. It's a little addictive so beware.

6 cups (1.5 L) onions, sliced into rounds about 1/8-in (2-mm)
  thick
1 stalk celery, minced
4 cloves garlic, minced
1/4 cup (60 mL) butter
1/4 cup (60 mL) olive oil
2 tsp (10 mL) salt
2 tsp (10 mL) pepper
1/2 cup (125 mL) flour
1 cup (250 mL) chicken or vegetable stock
2 cups (500 mL) milk
1/2 cup (125 mL) heavy cream (35% m.f.)
1 cup (250 mL) grated gruyere cheese
1 cup (250 mL) grated smoked Applewood cheddar
3 lb (1.5 kg) cooked and diced Yukon Gold potatoes, skins on
4 tbsp (60 mL) butter
1 cup (250 mL) breadcrumbs
4 tbsp (60 mL) butter

In a large saucepan, caramelize onions, celery, and garlic in butter and oil for 90 minutes (add the salt and pepper at this stage as well to bring out the water in the onions). Begin on high heat and reduce the heat to low for the most of the cooking time. Stir often with a wooden spoon, scraping the caramelized bits pieces from the bottom of the pan. The onions should be sweet and sticky and not look wet.

Add the flour to onions to form a roux and then add cold stock, milk and cream to the onion/roux mixture, stirring well. Simmer the sauce for 10 minutes on low. Add the cheeses and pour over the cooked diced potatoes in a casserole dish or large baking pan.

In a small non-stick pan, heat butter and toast breadcrumbs for a few minutes. Sprinkle over potato gratin and bake in a 350° F (180°C) oven for 40 minutes.

Serves 6 to 8

Desserts

We do not need desserts to live, but they sure make life worth living. Just the mention of a special dessert can define a cultural experience, such as a slice of Sachertorte in Vienna, or sticky toffee pudding in foggy London town. Few people do not enjoy dessert, although often we do not have a chance to enjoy it enough, as we are well and truly "packed" from the dishes that preceded the finale.

For me, dessert is a way to be sinful and to treat my guests, either at work or at home, to something that brings pure satisfaction. And I have always been keenly interested in creating new dishes that seem oddly familiar to the recipient.

The role of the great pastry chefs of the world is to wow us with spun sugar decorations, towers of chocolate and ornate plate designs. I am not a great pastry chef, and I believe that such grand creations are not achievable by the average cook, but I also believe that many excellent less-grand desserts are achievable.

Among the following dishes there are some new versions of classic recipes that we all know and love, but there are a few surprises as well. Be a little adventurous when dealing with your sweet tooth. The reward can be simply divine.

Maple Ice Cream

Using maple syrup in ice cream reminds me of drizzling it over snow, as native Canadians did centuries ago. The coolness on the palate diminishes the overbearing sweet sensation and allows the caramel/vanilla flavours to emerge. It is simple to make if you have an ice cream maker, and it works well with apple pie or angel food cake, or on its own.

4 cups (1 L) heavy cream (35% m.f.)
2 cups (500 mL) whole milk (4% m.f.)
2 tbsp (30 mL) maple extract
10 free-range egg yolks
2 cups (500 mL) Grade B or amber maple syrup
4 tbsp (60 mL) glucose syrup

In a heavy-bottomed saucepan, scald cream, milk and maple extract. In a mixing bowl, thoroughly combine egg yolks, maple syrup and glucose. Temper this mixture with the hot cream, one ladle at a time, stirring continuously. When all the cream has been added to the eggs, place this bowl over a pot of simmering water and cook while stirring with a rubber spatula. The eggs will cause the custard to thicken. When custard coats the back of a spoon, refrigerate until it is very cold. Churn this cold base in an electric ice cream maker, following the manufacturer's instructions. Store churned ice cream in a 4-pint (2-L) plastic container in the freezer for a minimum of 2 hours before serving.

Yields 2 litres

Upside-down Rhubarb Cake with Strawberry Rhubarb Sauce

Like a grandfather who gets up before sunrise, rhubarb is first up in the spring. It is most commonly used in sweet desserts like this one. Strawberries are not in season when rhubarb first appears, so I tend to raid my freezer for a bag of last year's crop. But I use fresh rhubarb rather than frozen — the frozen variety gives off too much water when the cake bakes.

Cake
2 cups (500 mL) white sugar
½ cup (125 mL) water
juice of ½ lemon
6 cups (1.5 L) diced fresh rhubarb
1 lb (450 g) butter
9 eggs
3 cups (750 mL) white sugar (second amount)
1 tbsp (15 mL) pure vanilla extract
2 cups (500 mL) unbleached flour

Strawberry rhubarb sauce
3 cups (500 mL) frozen strawberries
2 cups (500 mL) fresh or frozen rhubarb
1 cup (250 mL) white sugar
½ cup (125 mL) port wine *or* sweetened pure cranberry juice
½ tsp (1 mL) allspice
⅛ tsp (0.5 mL) salt
juice of ½ lemon

For the cake: In a heavy-bottomed saucepan, combine white sugar, water and lemon juice and bring to a boil. Cook over high heat until sugar caramelizes and begins to turn golden brown. Monitor the temperature with a candy thermometer. When sugar reaches 260°F (125°C), pour it into a parchment-lined rectangular 10 x 14-in (25 x 35-cm) cake pan. Spread sugar evenly over the bottom of the pan and cover with diced rhubarb. Set pan aside.

Brown the butter in a saucepan over medium-high heat until it foams, begins to change colour and smells "nutty." Stir butter as it cooks. When it is the colour of maple syrup, remove from the heat and set aside to be added to the cake batter.

Using an electric mixer, whisk together eggs, second amount of sugar and vanilla until the mixture is thick and makes "ribbons" when the batter falls from the whisk into the bowl. Gently fold in flour, then fold in the cooled but still liquid browned butter. Pour batter into the cake pan containing the caramel and fruit and bake in a 350°F (180°C) oven for 35 to 45 minutes or until the centre is set. Remove from the oven and allow to cool to room temperature.

For the strawberry rhubarb sauce: Combine all ingredients except lemon juice in a pot and bring to a simmer. Cook for 45 minutes on low heat then purée in a blender or food processor. Stir in lemon juice at the end. Refrigerate in a sealed container until needed.

To present the cake, run a paring knife along the inside of the pan and turn cake out onto a large platter. It should fall out easily due to the parchment paper on the inside. Cut into pieces 3 in (7.5 cm) square and serve with strawberry rhubarb sauce and whipped cream.

Makes 12 servings

Plum Tartlet with Brown Sugar Ice Cream

This dessert comes straight from a hotel pastry shop in Switzerland where I made the base tartlet with every fruit imaginable, about a thousand times over. When my father began growing his own plums I resurrected the recipe from my "little black book" and paired it with a simple brown-sugar ice cream.

Plum tartlet

½ cup (125 mL) white sugar
¼ tsp (1 mL) sea salt
2 tbsp (30 mL) unbleached flour
1 whole free-range egg
3 free-range egg yolks
¾ cup (180 mL) heavy cream (35% m.f.)
2 tbsp (30 mL) kirsch
1 tsp (5 mL) pure vanilla extract
Sweet Tartlet Dough (see recipe in "Basics" chapter)
16 small ripe plums, unpeeled and quartered
Brown Sugar Ice Cream (recipe follows)

Brown sugar ice cream

4 cups (1 L) heavy cream (35% m.f.)
2 cups (500 mL) whole milk (4% m.f.)
⅛ tsp (0.5 mL) freshly grated nutmeg
8 free-range egg yolks
1 ½ cups (375 mL) packed brown sugar
1 tbsp (15 mL) molasses

For the plum tartlet: In a mixing bowl, combine sugar, salt and flour. In a separate bowl, mix eggs, yolks, cream, Kirsch and vanilla. Combine with flour mixture and whisk until smooth.

Grease and flour a 10-in (25-cm) tart pan. Roll Sweet Tart Dough into a large round, about ⅛-in (3-mm) thick and line the pan with the pastry, trimming the edges of any excess. Cover the bottom of the pan with quartered plums, arranging them in concentric circles working from the outside inwards. Pour the batter in and around the plums, allowing some of the fruit to show through. Bake at 350°F (180°C) for 30 to 40 minutes.

Cut pie into wedges and serve immediately with a generous helping of Brown Sugar Ice Cream.

Serves 8

For the ice cream: In a saucepan, scald cream, milk and nutmeg. In a mixing bowl, whisk together egg yolks, brown sugar and molasses until smooth. Temper egg-and-sugar mixture with the hot cream one ladle at a time, stirring continuously. Place the mixing bowl containing the custard base over a pot of simmering water and cook, stirring continuously with a rubber spatula. When custard is thickened and will coat the back of a spoon, refrigerate until very cold. Churn the ice cream in an electric ice cream maker until smooth, following manufacturer's instructions. Store in a 4-pint (2-L) plastic container. The ice cream will require several hours in the freezer before it is hard enough to be scooped.

Yields 2 litres

Preserved Cherry Clafoutis

Although our global economy has given us access to fruits and vegetables from all over the world at any time of the year, often the quality is very poor. By preserving fruits when they are in season and perfectly ripe, we can also cook year-round with only minor adjustments to the way we would prepare fresh fruit. In this case, the preserved cherries will be wet and will need to be well-drained before combining with the batter.

2 cups (500 mL) preserved cherries (any type will do), strained and liquid reserved
1 oz (30 mL) kirsch
2 tsp (10 mL) cornstarch
3 tbsp (45 mL) white sugar
1 cup (250 mL) unbleached flour
3 free-range eggs
¼ cup (60 mL) brown sugar
1 tbsp (15 mL) pure vanilla extract
1 tsp (5 mL) baking powder
¼ tsp (1 mL) salt
1 ¼ cups (310 mL) milk
2 tbsp (30 mL) melted butter
¼ cup (60 mL) icing sugar (for garnish)

In a small bowl, combine cherries and kirsch and macerate for as long as possible, but at least 1 hour. Mix cornstarch and 1 tbsp (15 mL) of the cold cherry–preserving liquid in a separate bowl to form a slurry. In a small saucepan, bring liquid from the cherries and 3 tbsp (45 mL) of sugar to a boil and reduce until 1 cup (250 mL) of liquid remains. Pour kirsch off the cherries into the hot liquid and whisk in cornstarch slurry. The sauce will thicken. Allow to cool and refrigerate until needed.

To make the batter, mix flour, eggs, brown sugar, vanilla, baking powder and salt together in a bowl until smooth. Slowly add milk. Finally add butter, ensuring there are no lumps.

Spread cherries in a casserole dish or suitable ramekins in a single layer. Pour batter carefully over cherries but leave tops slightly visible. Bake at 350°F (180°C) until batter is set and slightly browned. Sprinkle with icing sugar before serving warm. Drizzle cherry sauce over the top of each portion.

Serves 10 to 12

Nova Scotia Ice Wine–Macerated Strawberries with Mint

Elegant and exceedingly simple, this dessert can only work when strawberries are perfectly ripe — never attempt it with off-season berries, and of course, buy local when you can. The presentation can be as simple or as complicated as you like. There is nothing wrong with coarsely chopping the berries and serving them in a bowl. I like to show off the beautiful symmetry of the fruit by fanning them on a plate. Either way, this dessert should be served with the same ice wine used in the dish.

1 qt (1 L) fresh strawberries
1 x 375-mL bottle Nova Scotian or other Canadian ice wine
2 tbsp (30 mL) white sugar
¼ cup (60 mL) small mint leaves

Hull strawberries using a sharp paring knife or hulling tool. Rinse gently under cold water, being careful not to bruise the fruit. Slice berries from top to bottom into 3 or 4 slices, depending on their size. Each slice should be about ¼ in (5 mm) thick. Place in a bowl with 3 oz (90 mL) of chilled ice wine and white sugar. Macerate fruit (soak in alcohol) for a minimum of 2 hours. Arrange slices of fruit in concentric circles on a small dessert plate and garnish with several tiny mint leaves.

Serve with a small glass of the remaining ice wine and some simple sugar cookies or pound cake, if desired.

Serves 4

Wildberry Napoleon with White Chocolate Mousse

There is a point every summer when the seasons for berries overlap, and that is the time to serve this elegant, light and delicious dessert. Success depends on the quality of the berries chosen and in being well organized. The crispy phyllo layers are easy to make but need to be watched carefully in the oven. The white chocolate mousse can be replaced with chocolate, strawberry or even a simple chantilly whipped cream if time is a factor. When all the elements are ready to go, assembling is fun.

Napoleon
1 package frozen phyllo dough
½ cup (125 mL) unsalted butter
¼ cup (60 mL) white sugar
1 cup (250 mL) highbush blueberries
1 cup (250 mL) raspberries
1 cup (250 mL) blackberries
1 ½ cups (375 mL) strawberries

Mousse
1 3/4 cups (425 mL) heavy cream (35% m.f.)
8 oz (225 g) white chocolate, finely chopped
1 tsp (5 mL) pure vanilla extract

For the napoleon: To prepare the crispy phyllo layers, allow frozen dough to thaw completely. Microwave butter until it is completely melted. Unfold dough and cover with a slightly dampened kitchen towel. Remove a single piece of dough and gently brush the entire surface with melted butter. Sprinkle about a teaspoon of granulated sugar over the buttered pastry and cover with a second piece of phyllo dough. Repeat the process two more times. Using a very sharp knife, trim the rough edges away. Cut the phyllo into two 4-inch (10-cm) pieces and place on a nonstick baking tray. Cover pastry with a piece of parchment paper and then a second baking tray that nests into the first. This will prevent the pastry from puffing up while baking. Bake at 350°F (180°C) for 8 to 12 minutes depending on the intensity of your oven. When pastry is golden brown, remove and allow to cool to room temperature. Do not refrigerate, or the pastry will become soggy.

For the white chocolate mousse: Bring ¾ cup (180 g) cream to the boil and pour over white chocolate in a mixing bowl. Stir until a smooth ganache forms, then cool on the countertop. When mixture is cool, whisk vigorously by hand or in a stand-up mixer until light and airy. In a separate bowl, whip remaining cream and vanilla to a "soft peak" stage. Gently fold one-third of the whipped cream into the chocolate, then another third and then the final third, being careful not to lose the light, airy texture. Fill a piping bag with a star tip attached and refrigerate for 30 minutes prior to use.

To serve the dessert, place a small dollop of mousse in the centre of a plate (this will prevent the dessert from sliding around on the plate). Place a crisp phyllo rectangle on the mousse. To prepare the berries simply wash them under cool water and rest on a paper towel to dry. Assemble the napoleon using a mixture of berries and several rosettes of white chocolate mousse. Use 3 pieces of phyllo per serving. Garnish with fresh mint, crème anglais, or a dusting of powdered sugar.

Serves 6

Rustic Red Haven Peach Tartlet

Red haven peaches are the ones grown in my family's orchard in Nova Scotia, but you can use any variety as long as they are ripe and in season. I call this tart rustic for two reasons. First, the pastry is simply wrapped around a small pile of peaches, giving it a homestyle look. Second, the filling has just three ingredients: peaches, sugar and cardamom.

8 ripe peaches
1 cup (250 mL) white sugar
1 tbsp (15 mL) ground cardamom
Flaky Pie Dough (see recipe in "Basics" chapter)
2 egg yolks
1 tbsp (15 mL) milk
2 tbsp (30 mL) coarse sugar, optional

To peel peaches, cut a small "X" in the bottom (opposite end to the stem). Blanch each peach in boiling water for 20 seconds and then plunge into an ice bath. The skins can then be removed easily with a small paring knife without losing any of the wonderful flesh. Cut peaches in half and remove stones. Then slice each half into 4 smaller pieces and place in a bowl. Toss peaches gently with sugar and cardamom. Portion Flaky Pie Dough into small 3-oz (90-g) balls. Using a rolling pin, roll each ball on a lightly floured work surface into 9-in (23-cm) rounds of pastry. Place a heaping pile of peaches in the middle of each pastry round and fold the sides up and around the fruit leaving a 1 ½-inch (4-cm) venting hole in the top.

In a small dish, mix egg yolks and milk. Use a pastry brush to spread mixture all over the finished tartlets. Sprinkle with a little coarse sugar and bake in a 350°F (180°C) oven for 35 to 40 minutes, or until crust is golden brown on the bottom.

To serve the tartlet, cut in half and garnish with some fresh peach slices and your favourite ice cream. The tart is shown here with homemade Maple Ice Cream (page 142).

Makes 6 tartlets

French Chocolate Ganache Torte with Raspberries

This is my *almost* flourless chocolate cake. It is extremely rich and should be served at room temperature. It is like eating a chocolate truffle, and therefore goes very well with the tart fresh raspberries.

Torte

9 oz (270 g) bittersweet chocolate (70% cocoa solids or higher)
1 cup (250 mL) unsalted butter
scant ½ cup (115 to 120 mL) white sugar
2 tbsp (30 mL) Grand Marnier or other orange liqueur
5 eggs
1 tbsp (15 mL) all-purpose flour

Ganache

5 oz (150 g) semi-sweet chocolate
2 tbsp (30 mL) heavy cream (35% m.f.)
2 tbsp (30 mL) unsalted butter
1 ½ tbsp (22 mL) Grand Marnier or other orange liqueur

Garnish

1 pint of fresh raspberries
whipped cream, optional

For the torte: Preheat oven to 350°F (180°C) and grease a 9-in (23-cm) springform pan with a little butter or sprag fat. Cut a round of parchment paper the same size as the bottom of the pan and position in the pan, also with a little butter on the surface. Finally, cut a piece of aluminum foil larger than the dimensions of the pan. Set the pan on top of the foil and fold the edges of the foil up and over the seal at the bottom of the springform pan. This will seal the pan and prevent water from getting into the pan later when the cake bakes in the water bath.

Using a double boiler melt bittersweet chocolate, butter and sugar together until smooth and silky. When melted, add liqueur of choice and set aside to cool slightly. (This can be done very carefully in a microwave, but I prefer to always melt chocolate in a mixing bowl over a pot of simmering water.)

In a separate bowl, or by using a stand-up mixer, beat eggs for 1 minute, until they become frothy. Add flour and mix well. Fold egg mixture into melted chocolate and then pour batter into the prepared springform pan. Set this pan into a large roasting pan and pour hot water into the roasting pan to surround the cake pan. The water level should be the same as the level of the chocolate. Bake for 25 to 30 minutes or until the centre of the cake is set. This can be tested using a toothpick or metal skewer. Remove cake from the water bath and cool on an elevated rack.

For the ganache (chocolate glaze): Simply melt semi-sweet chocolate, cream and second amounts of butter and liqueur together in a double boiler, stirring continuously until smooth.

When cake is cool to the touch, carefully remove the springform sides so the cake is exposed on all sides. Place cake back on the resting rack and pour the ganache over the top. Spread glaze all over the top and allow any excess to fall through the resting rack away from the cake. The cake can now be refrigerated until required.

Garnish with fresh raspberries, whipped cream or a little raspberry liqueur.

Serves 8

Wild Blueberry Biscuit Pudding with Lemon Curd

Although blueberries appear in late summer, they are the ultimate freezer fruit. Easy to use in muffins and desserts in their frozen form, they add nutrition and warm-weather flavour to so many recipes. The biscuits used here can be replaced with any type of good-quality bread like brioche, raisin bread or oatmeal brown. The term "wild" is loosely used to described small, lowbush blueberries as opposed to the larger, highbush variety.

Pudding

3 eggs
1 ½ cups (375 mL) coffee cream (18% m.f.)
zest of 1/2 lemon
1 tbsp (15 mL) pure vanilla extract
¾ cup (180 mL) brown sugar
1 tbsp (15 mL) chopped tarragon, optional
4 cups (1 L) diced dry tea biscuits
2 cups (500 mL) frozen lowbush blueberries
¼ cup (60 mL) melted butter
3 tbsp (45 mL) brown sugar (second amount)

Lemon curd

6 large free-range eggs
⅔ cup (170 mL) white sugar
1 tsp (5 mL) vanilla extract
¼ tsp (1 mL) sea salt
zest of 2 lemons
1 cup (250 mL) freshly squeezed lemon juice (*not* store bought)
¾ cup (180 mL) cold unsalted butter, cut into small cubes

For the pudding: In a bowl, mix eggs, cream, lemon zest, vanilla, brown sugar and tarragon together. Fold in diced biscuits and allow to rest in the refrigerator for 1 hour. Fold in blueberries and melted butter and fill a loaf pan or several smaller ramekins with the finished custard mixture. Sprinkle second amount of brown sugar on top. Bake in oven at 300°F (150°C) in a water bath for 30 minutes or until the middle is set.

Spoon hot pudding onto a dessert plate if you have used a single loaf pan or baking pan. If you have made individual puddings allow each to cool slightly before attempting to remove them from their ramekins or moulds.

For the lemon curd: Whisk eggs, sugar, vanilla, salt and lemon zest together until pale yellow in colour. Add lemon juice and pour into a heavy-bottomed saucepan. Begin warming mixture over medium heat, then reduce the heat to low as the temperature increases. When the mixture begins to thicken and takes on a pudding-like texture, remove from the direct heat and begin whisking in the butter, one cube at a time, until all is incorporated. Strain finished curd through a fine chinois or strainer to ensure there are no lumps. Place a piece of plastic film directly on top of the custard once it has been transferred to a suitable storage container. This will prevent a "skin" from developing while the curd is in the refrigerator.

To serve, warm each individual portion of blueberry pudding for a few seconds in the microwave. Place 2 heaping tbsp (35 mL) of lemon curd onto the centre of each plate. Place pudding on top of curd and garnish with fresh blueberries, mint or even a dollop of blueberry preserves.

Serves 8 to 10

Muscat-poached Pear and Goat Cheese Tartlet

If you want to make a "no-bake" cheesecake but prefer to "fancy it up" a little, this recipe is for you. The presentation is strikingly beautiful. I recommend garnishing this dessert with a few honey-roasted walnuts and serving it alongside a mild tea such as Darjeeling or a thyme-scented herbal variety.

Pears

1 x 750-mL bottle Muscat wine
2 cups (500 mL) white sugar
2 cinnamon sticks
6 whole cloves
4 medium-sized semi-ripe pears

Tartlets

⅓ cup (80 mL) unsalted butter
1 ¾ cup (430 mL) graham wafer crumbs
⅓ cup (80 mL) sugar
8 oz (225 g) creamy goat's cheese
½ cup (125 mL) white sugar
1 cup (250 mL) naturally thickened Greek yogurt
1 tbsp (15 mL) pure vanilla extract
2 gelatin leaves
1 1/4 cups (310 mL) whipping cream (35% m.f.)
2 tbsp (30 mL) white sugar (for brûlée crust on pears)

For the pears: Bring wine, sugar, cinnamon sticks, and cloves to a boil and reduce the heat to a simmering temperature of 140°F (60°C).

Peel each pear and cut in half, and use a teaspoon or melon baller to remove core. Place pear halves in the simmering liquid and cover with a circular piece of parchment paper the same diameter as the pot. Simmer pears for 20 to 25 minutes or until they are easily pierced with a small paring knife. Carefully remove pears from the poaching liquid with a slotted spoon and place on an elevated resting rack. Refrigerate until well-chilled.

In a saucepan, reduce poaching liquid by two-thirds, or until a sweet syrup remains. Set syrup aside to garnish the finished plate.

For the goat cheese tartlet shells: Grease and flour 8 x 4-in (20 x 10-cm) tartlet shells with removable bottoms. Melt butter in a saucepan or microwave and add graham crumbs and sugar. Combine well and press crumbs into each tart shell. Each crust should be approximately ¼-in (5-mm) thick. Bake shells in a 350°F (180°C) oven for 6 or 7 minutes until they set. Remove from the oven, cool and carefully remove shells from the moulds.

In a bowl, combine goat's cheese and sugar, then add yogurt and vanilla. Beat until smooth.

Soak gelatin leaves in lukewarm water for 5 minutes until they soften. In the microwave warm ¼ cup (60 mL) of heavy cream and add soaked gelatin leaves. Stir until gelatin dissolves in cream. Add to goat's cheese mixture and whisk to combine.

In a separate bowl, whip remaining cream until it reaches the "stiff peak" stage. Fold one-third of the cream into the goat's cheese mixture, then another third and then the final third, being careful to retain the light, fluffy texture. Fill each pre-baked tart shell with the cheese filling and refrigerate for a minimum of 3 hours before serving.

To plate the dessert, pat each pear half dry with a clean paper towel. Beginning about ½ in (1 cm) below the stem end of each pear half, cut 5 slices in each, spacing them ¼ in apart, ensuring that the stem end remains intact. Gently press down and to the side with your fingers, creating a "fan" effect. Place one fanned pear on top of each goat cheese tartlet. Sprinkle pear with about ½ tsp (3 mL) of sugar and caramelize the sugar using a blowtorch or crème brûlée torch. Garnish each tartlet with some fresh mint and a drizzle of the pear-poaching liquid reduction.

Orchard Oaks Riesling-poached Fruit with Star Anise Crabapple Sorbet

The inspiration for this dessert is my father. In 2005 he began operating an orchard in Port Williams, Nova Scotia, as a hobby. Since then all the fruit in my restaurant, Chives Canadian Bistro, has come from Orchard Oaks. This is the ultimate orchard fruit dessert and is made especially Nova Scotian when poached in local wine.

Poached fruit
1 bottle (750 mL) Canadian Riesling
2 cups (250 mL) white sugar
1 vanilla bean, split
2 pods star anise
4 small pears
1 lemon
4 peaches
4 yellow plums
4 purple plums

Sorbet
2 cups (500 mL) crabapples, cut in half
2 large red apples, unpeeled and quartered
1 cup (250 mL) apple cider
1 tsp (5 mL) lemon juice
¼ cup (60 mL) sugar
1 tsp (5 mL) brandy

For the poached fruit: Bring wine, sugar, vanilla bean and star anise to a boil in a small soup pot and reduce by one-quarter. Lower the heat to a simmer and cover the pot.

Peel whole pears using a vegetable peeler. Leave the stem intact and allow a small amount of the pear skin to remain on the pear just below the stem, for visual appeal. Using a melon baller or a tiny espresso spoon, remove core of pear by carefully digging at the bottom of the fruit. When seeds are removed, drop pears into a container of water along with the squeezed lemon. This will prevent the fruit from oxidizing.

To peel the remaining fruit, bring a pot of water to the boil. Also, prepare an ice bath next to the stove. Cut an "X" on the bottom of each peach and plum, and blanch fruit in the boiling water for 20 seconds. Immediately remove fruit from the water using a slotted spoon and shock in the ice bath. Remove skins from each piece of fruit using a small paring knife. The skins should peel away easily and not damage the delicate flesh underneath. Once peeled, cut fruit in half and remove the stones.

Carefully lower each piece of fruit into the simmering syrup, using a slotted spoon. You can cut a piece of parchment paper into a round and set it on top to keep the fruit submerged in the liquid. Small plums will require about 8 minutes in the liquid, peaches about 10 and pears about 15, all depending on the state of ripeness. When each piece of fruit is tender and easily pierced with a small knife, remove from liquid and refrigerate until ready for use.

For the star anise crabapple sorbet: Combine all ingredients except brandy in a saucepan. Cook until apples become soft, about 30 minutes. Purée apple mixture in a blender and pass through a fine-meshed chinois or strainer. Refrigerate until cool. Add brandy and process in an electric ice cream maker, following the manufacturer's instructions. Freeze for a minimum of 3 hours before serving.

Serve fruit with a ball of sorbet and a drizzle of the wine syrup, if desired.

Serves 4

Autumn Apple Soup, Toasted Almond Meringues, Caramel Mousse and Amaretto

This dessert is really nothing more than homemade applesauce taken to another level. I even go so far as to simmer the two soups in two different pots, one with peels and one without, creating a lovely color difference when the dish is presented.

Apple soups
2 lb (1 kg) Gravensteins or your favorite heritage apple
1 cup (250 mL) white sugar
1 tsp (5 mL) ground cloves
2 cinnamon sticks
⅛ tsp (0.5 mL) salt
2 cups (500 mL) apple cider

Meringues
3 egg whites
⅛ tsp (0.5 mL) almond extract
½ cup (125 mL) granulated sugar
¼ cup (60 mL) icing sugar
⅓ cup (80 mL) toasted and ground almonds

Mousse
1 ½ cups (375 mL) white sugar
3 tbsp (45 mL) corn syrup
juice of ½ lemon
¼ cup (60 mL) water
1 cup (250 mL) heavy cream (35% m.f.)
¼ cup (60 mL) unsalted butter
1 tsp (5 mL) pure vanilla extract
2 gelatin leaves
2 cups (500 mL) heavy cream (35% m.f.) (second amount)
3 tbsp (45 mL) Amaretto liqueur (for garnish)

For the apple soup: Peel, core and quarter half of the apples and place them in a saucepan. Quarter and core but *do not peel* remaining apples and place them in a second saucepan. Divide all remaining ingredients equally between the two saucepans and bring each to a simmer. Cook for 30 minutes, or until apples begin to fall apart. Purée each soup in a blender until smooth and refrigerate until ready to serve. If soups are too thick due to water reduction, add a little more apple cider to obtain the correct consistency.

For the toasted almond meringues: Beat egg whites and almond extract using an electric mixer until soft peaks begin to form. Gradually add granulated sugar in a slow, steady stream and beat on high speed until stiff, glossy peaks are visible. In a separate bowl, blend icing sugar and almonds. Gently fold almond mixture into egg-white mixture.

Preheat oven to 225°F (110°C) and prepare a cookie sheet with a piece of parchment paper or a silicone baking mat. The meringues can be spooned or piped into small circles, ovals or "kisses" depending on the desired effect. Each should have a diameter of no more than 1 ½ to 2 in (3.5 to 5 cm). Bake meringues until they are crisp and slightly golden. This will take about 1 hour, depending on your oven. Meringues can also be baked at a higher temperature for a shorter period of time. The effect here is a deeper golden exterior and a chewy interior. Experiment with the temperature and timing to find your favorite texture — they are all equally delicious.

For the caramel mousse: Combine white sugar, corn syrup, lemon juice and water in a heavy-bottomed saucepan and bring to a boil. As the mixture begins to boil, use a pastry brush and a little water to remove any sugar crystals from the side of the pan. Boil until sugar begins to caramelize and take on a golden-brown colour. The temperature can be checked with a candy thermometer: when it reads 300°F (150°C), remove from the heat and slowly add 1 cup (250 mL) of heavy cream. The sugar will bubble up vigorously and give off a lot of very hot steam, so be careful. Add butter and vanilla and place the pot back on a medium-low heat until sauce is smooth and sugar crystals dissolve completely. When the sauce is completely smooth, remove ¼ cup (60 mL) of caramel sauce and set aside. This will be used to garnish the dessert later.

In a small bowl, soak gelatin leaves in lukewarm water until soft. Add them to the main caramel sauce (not the ¼ cup that was set aside), stir to combine and set the pot aside to cool to room temperature.

In a clean bowl, whip second amount of heavy cream to stiff peaks. Fold half the whipped cream into the cooled but still liquid caramel sauce. Gently fold remaining whipped cream into the mousse, retaining as much of the air in the cream as possible. Refrigerate mousse for a minimum of 2 hours before using in the dessert. To plate the dessert, choose large soup plates with a bowl at least 6 in (15 cm) in diameter. Using 2 ladles, spoon a full ladle of each soup simultaneously into the bowl. The soup made with peeled apples will be golden in colour and the one made with unpeeled apples will be rose-coloured. Place 2 almond meringues in the centre of the bowl, followed by a large spoonful of caramel mousse. Drizzle one teaspoonful of reserved caramel sauce over each dessert, along with a teaspoonful of Amaretto liqueur.

Serves 8 to 10

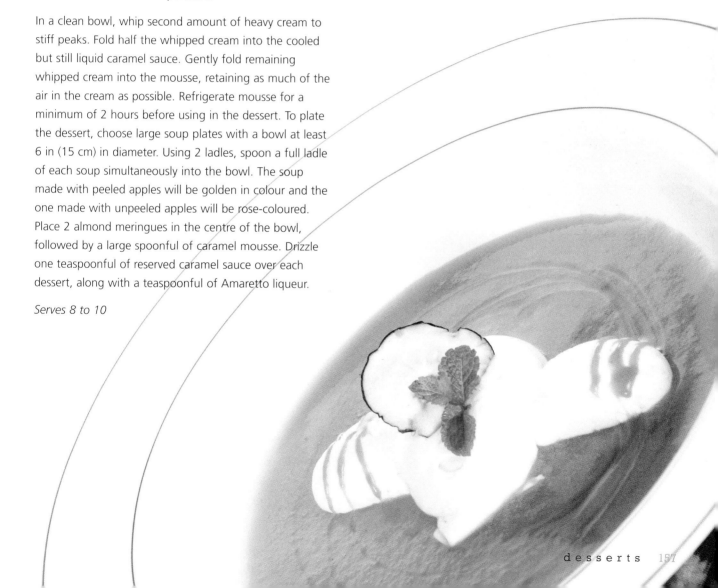

Acadian Sugar Pie

I love this recipe for its heritage, its flavour and its significance to the history of Canadian cooking. Except for the lemons and vanilla, these ingredients would have been available to our ancestors in the depths of winter. The fact that such a delicious and long-lasting dish has been crafted from just a few kitchen staples is, for me, the essence of cooking seasonally.

Sweet tartlet dough (see recipe in "Basics" chapter)
2 free-range eggs
2 free-range egg yolks
1 cup (250 mL) brown sugar
1 cup (250 mL) dark corn syrup or golden syrup
½ tsp (3 mL) sea salt
1 tbsp (15 mL) pure vanilla extract
juice of 1/2 lemon
½ cup + 2 tbsp (280 mL) unsalted butter

Grease a 10-in (25-cm) diameter tart pan and dust with flour, tapping out any excess. Roll the dough into a rough circle ensuring the crust is no more than ⅛ in (3 mm) thick. Place the dough into the shell and line the sides, pressing the dough into the scalloped edges of the tart pan. Cut away any overhanging dough. Using a fork, poke many holes (called "docking") in the bottom of the pan. Refrigerate until required.

In a bowl, beat eggs and egg yolks until slightly frothy. Add brown sugar, syrup, salt, vanilla and lemon juice and stir until well mixed and smooth. Melt butter in a microwave or small saucepan and add while hot to egg mixture. Pour filling into prepared tart pan. Bake at 350°F (180°C) for 35 to 40 minutes, depending on your oven, *or* until crust is brown and custard has set. The custard will never appear to be completely solid but will move as a semi-molten mass when the pan is agitated. Rest tart for 1 hour on the countertop to allow residual heat to finish cooking the centre, then refrigerate for a minimum of 3 hours before cutting for service.

Serve with a good dollop of unsweetened whipped cream and a few toasted nuts such as pecans, walnuts or hazelnuts to balance the dish — as the name implies, sugar pie is a very sweet dessert.

Serves 10

Fresh-ginger Gingerbread, Butterscotch Apples and Cinnamon Crème Anglaise

One of my personal favourites, hot gingerbread cake means *winter*. In the Maritimes everyone has a recipe, but most people would agree that the cake should be dark and moist. I like the heat created by using fresh ginger in my version. It gives a "snap" and spiciness in balance with the more subtle warmth of the powdered ginger.

Gingerbread
1 cup (250 mL) butter
1 cup (250 mL) brown sugar
6 free-range eggs
2 ½ cups (625 mL) molasses
4 cups (1 L) unbleached flour
1 ½ tbsp (22 mL) baking powder
2 tsp (10 mL) baking soda
4 tbsp (60 mL) cinnamon
3 tbsp (45 mL) ground ginger
3 tbsp (45 mL) grated fresh ginger
2 tsp (10 mL) ground cloves
½ whole nutmeg, grated
2 cups (500 mL) boiling water

Butterscotch apples
4 pie apples (Spy, Granny Smith or Jona Gold)
2 tbsp (30 mL) white sugar
1 tsp (5 mL) cinnamon
½ cup (125 mL) brown sugar
¼ cup (60 mL) butter
¾ cup (180 mL) golden corn syrup
1 small tin evaporated milk
2 tbsp (30 mL) Bailey's Irish Cream

Crème anglaise
4 egg yolks
¼ cup (60 mL) white sugar
1 tsp (5 mL) ground cinnamon
1 vanilla bean, split, with seeds scraped from pod
⅔ cup (170 mL) heavy cream (35% m.f.)
⅔ cup (170 mL) milk

For the gingerbread: Cream butter and brown sugar in an electric stand-up mixer or with a hand held unit. Gradually add eggs, then molasses and process until smooth. In a separate bowl sift together the dry ingredients. Fold into the wet ingredients and pour the batter into a large greased pan. Add the boiling water to this mixture and mix until just combined. It may be necessary to use two smaller pans as this recipe is quite large. Bake at 350°F (180°C) for 45 minutes or until the centre of the cake comes clean when a knife or cake tester is inserted.

For the butterscotch apples: Peel and core each apple and cut into eighths. Toss in white sugar and cinnamon and bake at 400°F (200°C) for 10 minutes, or until lightly browned. Set aside to cool. In a heavy-bottomed saucepan, cook brown sugar, butter, corn syrup and evaporated milk until it reaches the "soft ball" stage, 230°F (110°C) on a candy thermometer. Add Bailey's liqueur and stir in roasted apples.

For crème anglaise: Whisk egg yolks, sugar and cinnamon together in a mixing bowl until thick (the "ribbon stage"). In a saucepan, combine vanilla seeds and pod with cream and milk and heat *just below boiling*. Remove from the heat and temper egg-and-sugar mixture with 1 ladle of scalded cream at a time, stirring continuously. When all cream is added to eggs, pour mixture back into the saucepan and cook over very low heat for 10 to 15 minutes, or until the crème anglaise coats the back of a spoon. Strain the sauce through a fine-meshed chinois or strainer into a clean bowl sitting in a second bowl full of iced water. Stir sauce with a wooden spoon or rubber spatula as it cools in the ice bath. Do not use a whisk at this point or bubbles will form. Refrigerate sauce in a sealed container for up to 1 week.

Serve the dessert by warming the cake in a microwave for 20 to 30 seconds for each portion. Top with the apples and drizzle some of the cinnamon crème anglais on the plate. Garnish with a little whipped cream or vanilla ice cream if desired.

Serves 12

Warm Chocolate Cake with Bumbleberry Sauce

Molten chocolate cakes have been all the rage in restaurants for 10 years or so. These cakes can be baked just before you serve them, so that they have a molten interior. They can also be made in advance and more fully cooked, then reheated in the microwave.

Cake

8 oz (225 g) dark bittersweet chocolate
1 lb (450g) unsalted butter
5 eggs
4 egg yolks
½ cup (180 mL) white sugar
1 tbsp (15 mL) high quality vanilla extract
¼ cup plus 1 tbsp (95 mL) sifted cake flour
¼ tsp (1 mL) non-iodized salt
1 tbsp (15 mL) unsalted butter (second amount)
1 tbsp (15 mL) white sugar (second amount)

Bumbleberry sauce

1 cup (250 mL) blueberries
1 cup (250 mL) strawberries
½ cup (125 mL) raspberries
½ cup (125 mL) blackberries
1 cup (250 mL) white sugar
½ cup (125 mL) wild blueberry juice (apple or orange will work too)
1 tsp (5 mL) grated orange zest
⅛ tsp (0.5 L) salt

For the cake: Use a double boiler (a clean mixing bowl sitting over a pot of simmering water) to melt chocolate and first amount of butter together. When completely smooth set aside.

Combine eggs, egg yolks, first amount of white sugar and vanilla extract in a separate bowl in an electric stand-up mixer and mix with the paddle attachment until batter reaches the "ribbon stage." Whisk in melted chocolate and, when smooth, gently fold in flour and salt.

Using the second amounts of butter and sugar, grease and sugar the inside of 10 ramekins and fill ¾ full with chocolate batter. Refrigerate until batter has set. Preheat oven to 400°F (200°C) and bake for 10 to 12 minutes. Convection ovens may require a couple of minutes less. Remove from oven and rest cakes for 5 minutes.

For the bumbleberry sauce: Simmer all ingredients on low heat for 45 minutes. Thicken with a ½ tsp (3 mL) of cornstarch, if desired.

Remove cakes by running a small paring knife along the inside of each ramekin, then carefully turning the dish upside down in the middle of a serving plate. Do not move cake once it has been set in place or the liquid chocolate interior will run. Garnish with bumbleberry sauce, whipped cream or your favourite ice cream.

Serves 12

Chocolate Almond Biscotti

Almond flour is available commercially, but I prefer to make my own using fresh almonds as the pre-bought flour is often stale or even rancid. The chocolate and almond garnish is not absolutely necessary but certainly elevates the cookie from decent to extraordinary.

1 ½ cups (375 mL) whole peeled almonds
½ cup (125 mL) unsalted butter
¼ tsp (1 mL) salt
1 cup (250 mL) unbleached flour
1 cup (250 mL) cocoa powder
1 ¼ tsp (6 mL) baking powder
2 eggs
¾ cup (180 mL) white sugar
1 tbsp (15 mL) almond extract
6 oz (180 g) semi-sweet chocolate
2 tbsp (30 mL) unsalted butter (second amount)

Toast almonds in a 325°F (165°C) oven for 12 to 15 minutes, stirring once. They should obtain a golden colour and have a warm and nutty aroma. Allow almonds to cool completely before processing them into flour. This can be done using a food processor.

Place 1 cup (250 mL) of almond flour in a mixer and add first amount of butter and salt. (Reserve any remaining flour for garnish.) Using the paddle attachment, beat until smooth.

Sift together flour, cocoa powder and baking powder and set aside.

Whisk together eggs, sugar and almond extract until sugar dissolves. Mix dry ingredients into egg mixture and stir until smooth. Then add nut and butter mixture to the batter to make a soft cookie dough.

Prepare a cookie sheet with parchment paper or silicone mats, or by greasing and flouring the surface. Drop dough onto the cookie sheet and form into a long narrow log, about 1 in (2.5 cm) high and 4 in (10 cm) wide. Bake at 350°F (180°C) for 25 to 30 minutes. Allow baked loaf to cool for 30 minutes, then cut into individual biscotti-shaped cookies about 1in (2.5 cm) thick. Place cut biscotti on another cookie sheet and bake for an additional 15 minutes until they are toasted brown. Remove from the oven and cool the biscotti on an elevated rack.

When biscotti are completely cool, melt semi-sweet chocolate and second amount of butter in the microwave or in a double boiler until smooth. Dip one side of each biscotti into chocolate and set biscotti, chocolate side up, on a resting rack. Sprinkle a little reserved almond flour over chocolate while it is still wet. These biscotti can also be drizzled with a little white chocolate, as shown in the photo.

Makes 12 to 14 biscotti

Caramel Crème Brûlée with Chocolate Biscotti

Crème brûlée is a classic dessert that never grows old. Chocolate and caramel is a combination that stands above most other pairings in the dessert world, and this particular preparation goes very well with an exceptional coffee or cappuccino.

12 oz (375 g) white sugar
2 tbsp (30 mL) water
½ tsp (3 mL) lemon juice
2 cups (500 mL) heavy cream (35% m.f.)
1 cup (250 mL) milk
1 tbsp (15 mL) pure vanilla extract, or one vanilla bean, split
⅛ tsp (0.5 mL) salt
8 egg yolks
2 eggs
½ cup (125 mL) white sugar (for brûlée topping later)
Chocolate Almond Biscotti (recipe follows)

In a thick-bottomed and steep-sided saucepan, cook sugar, water and lemon juice until sugar caramelizes. If you feel unsure when the sugar is ready, use a candy thermometer to monitor the temperature. When it reads 290 to 300°F (145 to 150°C), carefully add cream and milk. *Be careful*, as adding the cream and milk is dangerous and can result in a burn from hot steam. Pour cream in first while standing away from the pot. Add milk next. The sugar will sizzle and spit quite a lot for a moment and then quieten down. When the liquid has settled, add vanilla and salt and bring to a boil to ensure all the sugar is melted.

In a separate bowl, whisk egg yolks and whole eggs together until combined. Slowly temper eggs with a ladle of hot cream, constantly stirring with a wooden spoon or whisk. When one-half of the hot cream is added, pour egg mixture back into the larger pot. Do not boil again, or the eggs will curdle. Pass the custard through a fine-meshed chinois or strainer.

Ladle custard into crème brûlée dishes no deeper than 1 ½ in (3.5 cm). Set the dishes in a pan, place the pan on the middle rack of the oven and add boiling water from a kettle to the pan. This will prevent the water from sloshing around and getting into the custard before it sets. Bake at 300°F (150°C) until just set in the middle. Ideally the custards will still be slightly "jiggly" in the middle when you remove them from the oven, as the residual heat will complete the cooking as they cool. Cool the crème brûlées in the refrigerator for several hours.

To serve, sprinkle about a teaspoon (5 mL) of sugar evenly over the top of each crème brûlée. Using a blowtorch, caramelize the sugar, being careful to do it as quickly as possible. This prevents the cool custard underneath from melting. Accompany each brûlée with a chocolate biscotti and a dollop of whipped cream, if desired.

Serves 6

Sticky Toffee Pudding

I began making this recipe in England during my apprenticeship. I strongly suggest making small individual puddings. You can use ramekins, muffin moulds or timbales — they all make for an elegant presentation. This dessert requires nothing but a little whipped cream or vanilla ice cream to finish.

1 lb (450 g) pitted dates
1 ¾ cups (450 mL) water
½ tsp (3 mL) salt
2 tbsp (30 mL) pure vanilla extract
6 ½ oz (180 g) softened unsalted butter
14 oz (400 g) brown sugar
¼ cup (60 mL) molasses or treacle
6 free-range eggs
½ cup (125 mL) milk
19 oz (530 g) flour
1 tbsp (15 mL) baking powder
1 tbsp (15 mL) butter
1 tbsp (15 mL) white sugar

Bring dates and water to a boil and simmer for 10 minutes. Purée mixture until very smooth and add salt and vanilla. Set aside to cool.

Cream the butter, sugar and treacle in a mixer using the paddle attachment until light and fluffy. Add cooled date purée and beat well. Add eggs, one at a time, along with small amounts of milk. When mixture is smooth, gently fold in sieved flour and baking powder. Grease 12 ramekins with butter and dust with sugar. Pour in batter and bake at 325°F (160°C) for 30 minutes.

Makes 12 puddings

English Toffee Sauce

This is an incredible match with the sticky toffee pudding. Sugar and butter boiled together create a nutty, butterscotch flavour. The method is quite unusual and takes some getting used to. Just follow the directions, don't panic, and you will be very happy with the results.

1 ¼ cups (300 g) white sugar
1 ¼ cups (300 g) unsalted butter
juice of 1 lemon
1 ¼ cups (300 g) heavy cream (35% m.f.)
1 tbsp (15 mL) pure vanilla extract
¼ tsp (1 mL) salt

In a heavy-bottomed saucepan, bring sugar and butter to a boil, stirring continuously. As the sugar cooks with the butter it will appear to "break," then foam up. Stir continuously and eventually the sauce will go smooth. At this point mix in lemon juice and cook for 1 minute. Remove sauce from the heat and add cream, vanilla and salt. Place sauce back on low heat and bring to a simmer. Keep sauce at room temperature before serving. Sauce should be kept sealed and in a cool area, but it is not necessary to refrigerate.

Yields 2 cups (500 mL)

Pickles & Preserves

When I was a kid I distinctly remember one day of every year, usually in September, when I was assaulted with the eye-watering pungency of vinegar and pickling spice in my mother's kitchen. It was chow day again. Now I too am a compulsive pickle-maker or "canner" and routinely stink up the kitchen at the restaurant. At 4 pm on pickle day, when the servers arrive, we always hear those familiar words, "What is that smell?"

Why is there a chapter on pickling and preserving in a book that is devoted to the use of fresh ingredients? The reason is that the real magic of canning is the ability to freeze time, so that foods are preserved for future use when they are at the peak of freshness. In February, the flavour of a jarred ripe tomato is usually far better than a "fresh" one bought from the store. Italian cooks have known this for a very long time — out of season they will always choose a canned plum tomato over an under-ripe one.

Pretty much anything can be preserved in a jar if the proper techniques are followed for sterilization. In the Maritimes, chow-chow, mustard pickles and bread and butter pickles — all recipes you will find in this chapter — are the condiments of choice for simple fish dishes, boiled dinners or cold meats.

Even the smallest city garden can yield enough produce for many jars of homemade history, allowing you to claim, "I grew those tomatoes!" at any time of the year.

Caesar's Asparagus (Pickled Asparagus)

I call this recipe Caesar's Asparagus for two reasons. First, it makes a fantastic garnish to the classic Caesar instead of celery. Second, the white balsamic vinegar, a unique Italian ingredient, adds more flavour to the recipe than just plain white vinegar. Pickled asparagus will accompany prosciutto, cold meats and seafood very well, as showcased in this book with a dish of Whole Poached Salmon (page 86).

5 lb (2 kg) asparagus
16 cups (4 L) boiling water
4 tbsp (60 mL) salt
1 ½ cups (375 mL) white balsamic vinegar
1 ½ cups (375 mL) water (second amount)
4 tbsp (60 mL) white sugar
½ cup (125 mL) minced shallots
3 cloves garlic, sliced
1 tsp (5 mL) yellow mustard seeds
2 tbsp (30 mL) cracked black peppercorns
1 tsp (5 mL) pickling salt
4 large sprigs fresh dill
4 bay leaves

Prepare four 500-mL Mason jars by boiling them for 5 minutes. Carefully remove from water and set aside. Cut asparagus to the height of the mason jars just below the neck (about 4 inches 10 cm, depending on the variety of jar you have). In a large pot, bring water and salt to a boil and blanch asparagus for 3 minutes. Cool quickly in iced water.

Wearing sterile latex gloves place blanched and chilled asparagus into the jars with the tender tips pointing up. In a separate pot, combine vinegar, water, sugar, shallots, garlic, mustard seeds, peppercorns and pickling salt and bring to a boil. Place a sprig of fresh dill and 1 bay leaf in each jar with the asparagus. Pour hot vinegar mixture over asparagus in each jar. Seal with sterilized lids.

Yields 4 x 500-ml Mason jars

Pickled Red Onions

These pickled red onions find their way into numerous vinaigrettes, condiments, salads and even sandwiches. Their colour is lovely and the taste is tangy and sweet, without any "oniony" aftertaste. I suggest having them on hand at all times as they are really simple to prepare and can be made year-round.

2 lb (1 kg) red onions
1 cup (250 mL) red wine vinegar
1 cup (250 mL) white sugar
1 bay leaf
1 tsp (5 mL) cracked black peppercorns
2 tbsp (30 mL) grenadine
1 tsp (5 mL) salt

Peel and thinly slice onions into rings about ⅛ in (3 mm) thick. In a pot, bring vinegar, sugar and all remaining ingredients to a boil. Pack onions tightly into Mason jars and pour hot liquid over the top. Seal when still hot and refrigerate for up to 1 month. For long-term storage, first sterilize the Mason jars in boiling water. Seal with sterilized lids, then boil each jar for 10 minutes, using a canning rack.

Yields 2 x 500-mL Mason jars

Quince and Raisin Chutney

Quince are a little hard to come by, certainly in grocery stores, but many apple growers also grow small quantities of quince for jellies and preserves. Ask around at your local farmers' market and put your order in with one of the growers. Quince can be used like apple in many recipes, but it must be cooked — it is hard and extremely tart on its own.

2 lb (1 kg) quince, peeled and diced
1 cup (250 mL) raisins
2 cups (500 mL) apple cider
1 cup (250 mL) freshly squeezed orange juice
zest of 2 oranges
3 cups (750 mL) diced sweet Vidalia onions
1 cup (250 mL) apple cider vinegar
1 cup (250 mL) brown sugar
2 tsp (10 mL) salt
1 tsp (5 mL) ground clove
¼ tsp (3 mL) cayenne pepper
1 tbsp (15 mL) yellow mustard seeds
1 tsp (5 mL) dried ginger
½ cup (125 mL) grated fresh ginger

In a pot, combine all ingredients and bring to a boil. Reduce heat and simmer for 2 hours or until all the liquid evaporates and the chutney becomes sticky in appearance.

For longer storage, sterilize three 500-mL Mason jars by boiling them for 5 minutes. Fill each jar with chutney. Melt preserve wax in a saucepan and pour over the top of the jarred chutney. Seal with a sterilized mason jar lid and store in a cool, dry place until required.

Yields 3 x 500 mL Mason jars

Chives' Mustard Pickles

This recipe was developed after much experimentation and taste-testing dozens of types of mustard pickles from village markets all over Nova Scotia. It has evolved into a spoonable chutney-style pickle, rather than the large, chunky variety. It works well as a garnish for fish or as a condiment with burgers and sausages.

10 cups (2 ½ L) diced and seeded English cucumbers (see instructions)
¾ cup (180 mL) rock salt
5 cups (1.25 L) boiling water
5 cups (1.25 L) diced onions
1 cup (250 mL) minced red pepper
1 cup (250 mL) minced green pepper
4 stalks celery, minced
3 tbsp (45 mL) whole yellow mustards seeds
4 tbsp (60 mL) dry mustard
4 tbsp (60 mL) turmeric
1 tbsp (15 mL) crushed fenugreek
1 tbsp (15 mL) cumin
2 tbsp (30 mL) ground black pepper
6 cups (1.5 L) white vinegar
8 cups (2 L) white sugar
1 cup (250 mL) cornstarch

To properly prepare cucumbers, slice lengthwise and, using a spoon, remove pulpy seeds from the centre. Do not peel. Dice into pieces about ½-in (1-cm) square. Add salt to water and bring to a boil. Pour salted water over cucumbers, onions, peppers and celery and let stand for 2 hours. Drain and set aside.

In a large pot, combine spices with vinegar and sugar. When thoroughly mixed remove 2 cups (500 mL) and set aside. Add vegetables to the pot and bring to a boil. Reduce heat to medium and cook for a minimum of 15 minutes to remove as much excess water from the vegetables as possible. Make a slurry of cornstarch and reserved vinegar/sugar blend. Increase the heat again to high and resume the boil. Add cornstarch slurry and stir continuously until pickles and sauce thicken. Simmer for 3 minutes and proceed to jarring in sanitized containers. It is always best to follow the manufacturer's directions for sterilizing Mason jars and lids.

Yields 7 to 8 litres or 15 X 500-mL Mason jars

Apple, Cranberry and Star Anise Chutney

Perfect with turkey, succulent chicken pot pie or Acadian tourtière, this cranberry accompaniment can be spiced up with a few dashes of hot sauce or even some fresh ginger, but I prefer to allow the star anise to come through. This licorice-flavoured Asian spice brings out the natural flavours of meat dishes.

5 lb (2 kg) fresh or frozen cranberries
2 lb (1 kg) apples, peeled and diced
2 cups (500 mL) packed brown sugar
2 cups (500 mL) honey
2 cups (500 mL) apple cider vinegar
1 tsp (5 mL) ground clove
2 tsp (10 mL) salt
2 star anise pods, ground

Combine all ingredients in a pot and bring to a boil.
Simmer for 1 hour, or until chutney begins to look sticky,
not watery. Fill sterilized Mason jars with chutney and seal
with appropriate lids.

Yields 4 x 500-mL Mason jars

Green Tomato and Apple Chow

Chow-chow, as it is affectionately called in the Maritimes, is made with green tomatoes and onions. I use the apple as a sweetening element. It is crucial to use an apple that holds its shape, otherwise it will melt and make the chow sloppy. I also cook my chow a bit less than other chefs, as I enjoy the crisp texture of the tomato and onions.

9 lb (4 kg) green tomatoes, diced
2 lb (1 kg) onion, diced
¼ cup (60 mL) rock salt
2 lbs (1 kg) peeled and diced apple (Jona Gold or Northern Spy)
2 cups (500 mL) apple cider vinegar
1 ½ cups (375 mL) brown sugar
1 tsp (5 mL) cloves
1 tsp (5 mL) ground black pepper
½ tsp (3 mL) allspice
2 cinnamon sticks
1 tsp (5 mL) dry mustard
¼ cup (60 mL) pickling spice
2 tbsp (30 mL) cornstarch
3 tbsp (45 mL) water

In a large mixing bowl, combine green tomatoes, onions and rock salt and set in a cool place overnight. It is not necessary to refrigerate at this point, as you want to extract as much water as possible from the vegetables. This process is more efficient if the vegetables are not extremely cold.

Drain released liquid from vegetables, but do not rinse. Place vegetables in a large pot and add apples, vinegar, brown sugar and spices. The pickling spice, available as a mix in most grocery stores, is best wrapped in a sachet of cheesecloth. This bundle can then be easily removed after the pickles have simmered. Handy spice bags are now available as well during the pickling season.

Simmer pickles on low heat for 1 hour. Remove sachet and discard. Make a slurry of cornstarch and water and add to the pot. The sauce will thicken very slightly and develop a lovely glossy sheen. Jar the chow in sterilized Mason jars, following the manufacturer's instructions.

Yields 8 to 9 litres or approximately 16 x 500 mL
Mason jars

Basics

In this chapter you will find a resource of basic recipes that are needed to prepare some of the other dishes in this book. It also includes a few recipes that didn't fit elsewhere. These are not simple food concepts that are at the back of the book because they lack importance. They represent the building blocks of all great recipes. I spend most of my time in the kitchen finding top-notch base recipes.

The very first lesson that a culinary student is taught is how to make a proper stock. Stocks form the foundation for rich sauces, soups, braises, pilafs, risottos and meat and vegetable broths. They are crucial for quality cooking. I am guilty of turning to the canister of powdered bouillon from time to time myself, but never for our restaurant sauces. The intricacy of flavour in a reduced beef broth is essential for a delicious demi-glace or succulent ragout.

No matter how creative a chef may be, these recipes — once learned — are always there, providing a firm basis for new ideas. With a wonderful pâté brisée recipe in your portfolio, that show-stopping fruit tart or a quiche for Mother's Day brunch lies within your grasp.

Maple Butter

Beautiful on biscuits, a piece of roasted trout or pancakes, maple butter is worth a little extra work for special occasions. Use salted butter as it gives a nice balance to the sweet syrup.

½ lb (225 g) salted butter
¼ cup (60 mL) amber (Grade B) maple syrup

Bring butter to room temperature. Whip butter and the maple syrup together until light and fluffy, about 5 minutes, using a tabletop or handheld mixer for best results.

To serve, fill a butter dish with maple butter and smooth over the top with a knife. Drizzle a few drops of maple syrup on the top to garnish.

Yields 2 cups (500 mL) whipped butter

Classic Risotto

This recipe acts as a vehicle for creativity in risotto making. Nearly any flavour imaginable can be added here, and risotto can be served as an accompaniment to almost any protein from beef to lamb, from chicken to seafood. And of course, substituting vegetable stock for chicken stock makes it vegetarian.

1 medium onion, minced
1 clove garlic, minced
½ stalk celery, minced
½ tsp (3 mL) salt
2 tbsp (30 mL) butter
2 tbsp (30 mL) extra-virgin olive oil
1 cup (250 mL) Italian Arborio or Caranoli rice
½ cup (125 mL) dry white wine or vermouth
3 ½ cups (875 mL) hot chicken or vegetable stock
½ cup (125 mL) grated Parmesan cheese

In a heavy-bottomed sauté pan, sauté onion, garlic, celery and salt in butter and oil over medium heat for 5 minutes, or until they are soft. Add rice and cook for 3 minutes on medium heat until the grains look translucent. Deglaze the pan with wine and cook until the bottom of the pan is dry. Begin adding hot stock 1 cup (250 mL) at a time, stirring constantly. The risotto will take about 15 to 18 minutes to cook depending on the variety of rice. When risotto is fully cooked but still *al dente* (the grain still gives some resistance when bitten) remove from heat and stir in Parmesan cheese. Serve immediately.

Serves 4

White Sauce

In classic cooking there are two "mother" sauces that can be used as bases for other sauces that are white: the *béchamel* and the *velouté*. Each is thickened using a roux, but the béchamel is milk-based and the velouté is stock-based. The term "white sauce" normally refers to a milk-based béchamel sauce, but the following recipe is a variation we use at Chives. It has both stock and cream as well as cheese. It works well for pastas, can be stirred into mashed potatoes to make them creamier and can be added to a cream soup at the end to enhance its richness. It is my version of a multi-purpose sauce that is always handy in our kitchen.

1 onion, minced
1 celery stalk, minced
2 cloves garlic, minced
¼ cup (60 mL) butter
¼ cup (60 mL) flour
½ cup (125 mL) white wine
4 cups (1 L) chicken stock
4 cups (1 L) whipping cream (35% m.f.)
2 bay leaves
2 sprigs fresh thyme
¼ cup (60 mL) Roasted Garlic Purée (see recipe in this chapter)
1 cup (250 mL) grated Parmesan cheese
1 tsp (5 mL) hot sauce

Sauté onion, celery and garlic in butter for 5 minutes. Add flour and stir to form a roux. Slowly add wine, then stock and finally the cream, whisking continuously. When a smooth sauce has formed, lower the heat and add herbs and the roasted garlic purée. Simmer for 30 minutes and strain. Add Parmesan cheese to strained sauce and season with hot sauce.

Yields 2 ½ L (2500 mL)

Aioli

Aioli is really a garlic mayonnaise and is a staple in Italian cooking. It is traditionally made in a mortar and pestle, the original food processor, but you can make it either in an electric food processor or by hand with a whisk. Choose garlic that is young and very fresh. Older garlic is dry and has a more fully developed germ in the middle. This germ contains bitter heat that gives the aioli an unpleasant taste.

5 cloves garlic, peeled, halved, and germ removed (if required)
4 large free-range egg yolks
¼ tsp (1 mL) salt
1 cup (250 mL) light olive oil
2 drops Tabasco sauce
½ tsp (3 mL) lemon juice
a few grindings of black pepper

Pulse garlic until well chopped. Add egg yolks and salt and purée on high for 30 seconds. Through the top hatch of the food processor add the oil in a slow and steady stream until a smooth sauce forms. When all the oil is added season with Tabasco, lemon juice and black pepper. Adjust salt if necessary.

Yields 1 ¼ cups (310 mL)

Pasta Dough

Many pasta recipes call for durum semolina flour. This is more common in dried pastas. I use regular flour for the simple reason that it is usually what I have on hand. Keeping pasta simple but following a couple of rules ensures good results. First, always allow the pasta to rest before processing it through a machine roller. Second, keep the dough covered with a dampish cloth to prevent it from drying out.

1 lb (450 g) flour
2 eggs plus 4 egg yolks
¼ tsp (1 mL) salt

Pile flour in the middle of your work surface and make a well in the centre. Combine eggs, yolks and salt in the well and, using a fork, begin whisking egg mixture. Slowly incorporate flour from the sides of the well into the mix. When mixture becomes too thick for the fork, use your hands and knead dough for 3 or 4 minutes until it is smooth.

It may not be necessary to always use all of the flour. Weather conditions and varieties of flour make a big difference. Experience will tell you when the dough is soft and moist enough but not so soft that it sticks to your hands. The best word to describe the feeling of the perfect pasta dough is "tacky."

Wrap dough in plastic film and set in the refrigerator for a minimum of 2 hours before use (overnight is best).

Makes 1 ½ lbs (650 g) dough

Chicken Stock

Good restaurants rely on flavourful stock for everything from soups to risottos. Meat purveyors know this, and that is why frozen chicken bones are priced ridiculously high. What used to be scrap now costs almost as much as a whole bird by weight. I use stewing hens instead of bones for stock. That way I can use the meat for pot pies, soups or simple lunches, so nothing is wasted. Many chicken-stock recipes call for the bones to be roasted, the correct procedure to maximize flavour when using bones and scraps of meat. I do not roast the hens, as I do not want the meat to become dry and less useful for other recipes.

2 stewing hens (about 6 lb or 2.7 kg each)
2 cups (500 mL) coarsely chopped onion
1 cup (250 mL) coarsely chopped white of leek
1 ½ cups (375 mL) coarsely chopped celery
1 ½ cups (375 mL) coarsely chopped carrot
4 bay leaves
3 sprigs fresh thyme
1 tbsp (15 mL) whole black peppercorns
cold water to cover (about 1 ½ gallons/6 L)

Cut hens into quarters and rinse well under cold water. Place all ingredients in a large stockpot with the chicken on top of the vegetables. This will make it easier to skim during the simmer. Cover with cold water (the water can rise about 1 in (2.5 cm) above the level of the chicken, but no more). Heat on high until the water boils and immediately reduce to a simmer. Cook for 3 hours, skimming any fat or scum from the top of the liquid. Strain stock through a chinois or colander and reserve. When the cooked chicken meat is cool to the touch it can be picked and used elsewhere.

Yields 8 cups

Maple Balsamic Syrup

This simple recipe has become a trademark flavour of my restaurant. We use it mostly as a garnish for soup, foie gras, terrines and the odd dessert, but it also acts as the *je ne sais quoi* in sauces and ragouts. I learned how to make this syrup from an experiment years ago with Michael Smith and have kept on making it. It is wonderful stuff.

2 cups (500 mL) cooking-grade balsamic vinegar (nothing too expensive)
1 cup (250 mL) amber (Grade B) maple syrup

In a saucepan, reduce vinegar by one-half. Add maple syrup and reduce by one-third. Cool completely and store in a food-safe garnishing bottle (available from a good kitchen supple store) or a used mustard bottle. The syrup should have the same consistency as loose molasses and can be adjusted by adding a few drops of water or reducing a little more over high heat.

Yields 1 ⅔ cups (430 mL)

Flaky Pie Dough

The most important thing to remember in obtaining a perfect dough is to never touch the butter and have *everything* cold. Here the method of freezing butter first and grating it ensures the butter will be the perfect size. It also means the dough will remain colder longer, allowing pockets of butter to remain suspended in the flour, the key to a flaky pastry.

2 ½ cups (625 mL) unbleached white flour
1 tsp (5 mL) baking powder
½ tsp (3 mL) sea salt
1 cup (250 mL) frozen unsalted butter
½ to 3/4 cup (125 to 180 mL) iced water
1 egg yolk
1 tsp (5 mL) white vinegar

Thoroughly combine flour, baking powder and salt in a mixing bowl. Remove butter from the freezer just before use and grate directly into the flour mixture using the large size of a box grater. In a separate bowl, mix iced water, egg yolk and vinegar together. Add to butter/flour mix and just bring together. Do not knead more than necessary. Wrap in plastic film and allow to rest for 90 minutes in refrigerator before using (overnight is best).

Yields 1 lb (450 g) dough

Sweet Tartlet Dough

I use this dough for tarts that do not have a top to the crust or that have a light filling. Because there is no egg or livener of any type this crust will not bubble and will bake evenly. This is ideal for the Acadian Sugar Pie and Plum Tart recipes in this book.

2 cups (500 mL) unbleached flour
½ tsp (3 mL) sea salt
1 tbsp (15 mL) white sugar
½ cup (125 mL) unsalted butter
½ to ¾ cup (125 to 180 mL) iced water

Sift flour, salt and sugar together in a mixing bowl. Using a fork, pastry cutter or a food processor, cut butter into the flour until mealy. Add ½ cup (125 mL) iced water, then add a little more if necessary. Just combine with a fork, dump onto a lightly floured work surface, and knead only once or twice to form the dough. Cover and rest for 30 minutes in the refrigerator before use.

Yields 1 lb (450 g) dough

Vegetable Stock

Writing a recipe for vegetable stock is a difficult task, as the stock usually gets the trimmings from many varieties of vegetables. Tomato pulp, cucumber peel, zucchini ends and even onion peels can be used in stocks to avoid waste. A few standard choices should always be in the pot, but feel free to add anything you have available, with the exception of beets, which will obviously discolour the liquid, and potatoes, which add little flavour and will cloud the broth.

2 lb (1 kg) coarsely chopped onion
1 lb (450 g) coarsely chopped carrot
1 lb (450 g) coarsely chopped celery
1 lb (450 g) coarsely chopped anise bulb
½ lb (225 g) white of leek, cleaned and chopped
2 cloves garlic
¼ cup (60 mL) light olive or vegetable oil
1 tsp (5 mL) salt
4 sprigs fresh thyme
½ bunch Italian parsley
2 sprigs fresh sage
6 bay leaves
1 tbsp (15 mL) whole black peppercorns
1 gallon (4 L) cold water

Sauté onion, carrot, celery, anise, leek and garlic in oil and add salt. The salt will help release some of the flavour but will not be enough to make the stock salty. Add herbs and spices and cover with cold water. Bring to a simmer and cook for 45 minutes. Strain and refrigerate or freeze stock in small amounts immediately.

Yields 4 litres (1 gallon)

Chive Olive Oil

Also known as "green oil" in my kitchen, chive olive oil is pretty much the only modern fancy food garnish I use. I like being able to add the essence of chive and fresh onion to a plate, as well as a lovely colour. It works best in soup, as the fragrant oil becomes mixed with the broth and other complementary flavours as it is eaten spoonful-by-spoonful.

2 cups (500 mL) green leek tops, well cleaned
1 bunch fresh chives
½ cup (125 mL) light olive oil

Purée ingredients in a blender. Place in a small saucepan and slowly warm over medium heat. As the mixture heats the fibrous materials will begin to coagulate and the oil will separate. Cook for about 10 minutes until the mixture is hot, then strain through a coffee filter or cheesecloth. When the strained oil is cool transfer it into a squeeze bottle. Allow it to rest for several minutes. If water collects on the bottom turn the bottle upside down while plugging the hole with your finger. Wait a minute for the water to settle on the bottom and remove your finger. Gently squeeze the bottle to remove the water. When pure oil is visible stop squeezing and turn the bottle upright again.

Yields ½ cup (125 mL) or one small squeeze bottle

Chives' Buttermilk Biscuits

These are drop biscuits, not rolled and cut as many other recipes suggest. Little irregular edges in the dough brown and crisp while baking, giving the biscuit a lovely texture. This is the exact recipe we have served at Chives every night since we opened.

4 cups (1 L) unbleached white flour
4 tsp (20 mL) baking powder
4 tsp (20 mL) white sugar
½ tsp (3 mL) salt
½ lb (225 g) butter
3 free-range eggs
1 ¼ cups (310 mL) buttermilk

Mix flour, baking powder, sugar, and salt well in a large mixing bowl.

Using a fork or pastry cutter, cut butter into the dry ingredient mix until mealy in texture. In a separate bowl, beat eggs into buttermilk. Make a well in the centre of the dry ingredients and pour in beaten eggs and buttermilk. Using a fork, start combining the dry and wet ingredients by running the fork along the outside of the bowl down to the middle and then out. Spin the bowl a little each time and repeat this folding motion. This will prevent dry flour from remaining unmixed at the bottom of the bowl and incorporate all ingredients more quickly. Drop dough onto a nonstick baking tray using a spoon. Each ball of dough should be approximately 2 ½ in (6 cm) in diameter before baking. Preheat oven to 400°F (200 °C) and bake until golden brown (about 12 to 15 minutes).

Makes 18 to 20 biscuits

Roasted Garlic Purée

Recently garlic has become readily available in grocery stores in large bags up to 3 lb (1.5 kg), already peeled. Although a full head of garlic is easily roasted by placing in a 350°F (180°C) oven for 25 minutes, making a larger batch and freezing it in small portions makes more sense if you do a lot of cooking. It can be tossed frozen into a tomato sauce, soup or any braised dish to add a depth and sweetness of flavour that raw sautéed garlic cannot duplicate.

1 lb (450 g) peeled garlic
½ cup (125 mL) olive oil
¼ tsp (1 mL) salt
¼ tsp (1 mL) pepper

Toss all ingredients in a bowl and place on a nonstick baking dish about 9 x 12 in (22 x 30 cm) in size. Wrap in aluminum foil and use a knife to cut 3 small slits in the top of the foil. Roast in a 350°F (180°C) oven for 40 minutes, stirring garlic every 10 minutes. When garlic is light brown in colour and smells nutty and sweet, remove from the oven and strain away the excess oil. This oil can be reserved and used for sautéeing if desired. Purée garlic in a food processor until very smooth and freeze in ice-cube trays. The garlic purée will keep refrigerated for 2 weeks.

Yields 1 lb (450 g) purée

Pizza Dough

Simple pizza dough is really not that simple when you consider that there are probably thousands of recipes in existence, each using the same handful of ingredients in slightly different quantities. However, pizza is rustic Italian food and should never be stressed over. Slight imperfections will give your pizza charm, any lack of expertise creating a sense of adventure.

½ cup (125 mL) lukewarm water (about 105°F, 40°C)
1 tsp (5 mL) sugar
2 ¼ tsp (11 mL) dry yeast (1 envelope)
4 cups (1L) bread flour (plus a little extra for dusting)
2 tsp (10 mL) sea salt
1 ½ cups (375 mL) lukewarm water (about 105°F, 40°C) (second amount)
2 tbsp (30 mL) extra-virgin olive oil

In a small bowl, combine first ½ cup (125 mL) of lukewarm water with sugar and yeast. Stir and allow to sit for 20 minutes to activate the yeast.

In a larger bowl, combine bread flour and salt and mix well. Make a well in the middle of the flour mix and add fermenting yeast, second amount of lukewarm water and olive oil. Begin mixing with a fork, scraping the sides of the bowl well to pick up the flour. When the mixture becomes too thick for the fork, dump it onto a floured work surface and begin kneading. Add a few sprinkles of extra flour if the dough seems too sticky.

Knead dough for 10 minutes, until it is smooth and elastic to the touch and does not stick to your hands. Place in a floured or oiled bowl and cover with plastic film. Let rest for at least 30 minutes before using. Cut dough into 6- to 7-ounce (180- to 210-g) balls (for a 12-in/30-cm pizza) and wrap individually with cling film. The dough can be rested in the refrigerator until ready for use, or frozen in balls.

Makes 1 1/2 lbs (650 g) dough or enough for two 12 in to 14 in (30-35 cm) pizzas

Beef Stock and Demi Glace

Great beef stock is crucial for a great demi glace. Great demi glace is crucial for great meat sauces. And great meat sauces elevate simple dishes to something extraordinary. What my chef instructor said on the first day of culinary school was true: "Good cooking starts with the stock."

Simple beef stock
5 lb (2.25 kg) beef or veal bones
5 lb (2.25 kg) meaty soup bones
2 lb (900 g) coarsely chopped onion
1 lb (454 g) coarsely chopped celery
1 lb (454 g) coarsely chopped carrot
½ lb (225 g) white of leek, optional
1 large ripe tomato, coarsely chopped
2 cloves garlic
4 bay leaves
4 sprigs fresh thyme (or 2 tsp dried thyme)
½ bunch Italian parsley
2 tbsp (30 mL) whole black peppercorns
cold water to cover

Demi glace
¼ lb (110 g) butter
½ cup (125 mL) flour
1 lb (454 g) chopped onion
½ lb (225 g) chopped celery
½ lb (225 g) chopped carrot
2 cloves garlic
1 small tin (½ cup/125 mL) tomato paste
2 cups (500 mL) dry sherry or red wine
2 gallons (8 L) beef stock
2 bouquets garnis (2 sprigs fresh thyme, 2 bay leaves, bunch of parsley stems, all wrapped with a piece of green leek top and tied with a piece of butcher's twine)
salt and pepper

For the simple beef stock: Preheat oven to 350°F (180°C) and roast bones and vegetables until golden brown. Place bones in a large stockpot on top of vegetables. Drain off any excess fat from the roasting pan and deglaze with a little water, scraping any golden bits from the bottom of the pan. Add this to the stockpot, cover with cold water, and add all remaining ingredients. Heat on high until water just comes to a boil, then reduce the heat and simmer for 6 hours. Skim stock every 30 minutes using a ladle or serving spoon. Strain stock and refrigerate or freeze in smaller quantities.

Yields 2 gallons (8 L)

For the demi glace: Cook butter and flour together in the bottom of a stockpot until they turn dark brown in colour, about 30 minutes. Add onion, celery, carrot and garlic and cook for another 10 minutes. Add tomato paste and cook for a further 10 minutes. Add sherry and stir to combine. Add half the beef stock (1 gallon) and 1 bouquet garni and simmer for 1 hour, skimming as often as possible. Strain through a fine-meshed chinois or china cap.

The resulting sauce is known as a *Sauce Espagnole*, a classic base sauce used to make various rich meat sauces.

To complete the demi glace, add remaining beef stock to the *Sauce Espagnole* along with the second bouquet garni. Bring sauce to a boil and reduce by two-thirds. Skim frequently to remove any impurities from the sauce. The reduction will take about 2 hours. Season the finished demi glace with salt and pepper to taste.

Yields 12 cups (3 L)

Recipes for spring

Recipes for summer

Recipes for fall

Recipes for winter

Recipes for all seasons

Index

Photo Credits

l = left, r = right, t = top, b = bottom, c = centre

All interior photos by Alanna Jankov, except where noted below:
Silvia Cosimini: 62tc; Suzanna Diebes: 82c; Karen Feher: 82bl; Neco Garnica: 62br; Sanja Gjenero: 166br; Elisabetta Grondona: 62bl; Lotus Head: 82tl; Craig Jewell: 140tr, 140bc; Christa Richert: 140cl; Andrew Simpson: 140br; Emma W: 82bc; Wolfgang Wittmann: 82tr; Michal Zacharzewski: 166tr.

Craig Flinn and his mother, Faye Flinn.